the
new
gardener's
handbook

the new gardener's handbook

Everything You Need to Know to Grow a Beautiful & Bountiful Garden

Daryl Beyers

GARDENING INSTRUCTOR AT THE
NEW YORK BOTANICAL GARDEN

TIMBER PRESS · PORTLAND, OREGON

To Genevieve,
who prayed
for this book
to happen.

Photo and illustration credits appear on page 223.

Published in 2020 by Timber Press, Inc.

The Haseltine Building
133 S.W. Second Avenue, Suite 450
Portland, Oregon 97204-3527
timberpress.com

Printed in China
Text and cover design by Adrianna Sutton

ISBN 978-1-60469-874-9

Catalog records for this book are available from the
Library of Congress and the British Library.

contents

preface

The Science and Art of Gardening

I never set out to become a professional gardener. Gardening, quite simply, was the career that happened to me. My life with plants started while pursuing a college degree in environmental design, but I also learned from the ground up while working on landscape crews and at garden centers. After graduation I traveled the country making gardens for family, friends, friends of family, and family of friends—anyone who would let me dig holes in their yard. I even published some magazine articles on gardening, and when I landed a job as head gardener on a ten-acre estate, my life in gardening really began to flourish.

My mission, as I saw it, was to keep every plant in that garden alive, which was crazy. The first lesson every new gardener learns is that plants die. Second, try as we might, not every plant in our care will thrive. Since then I have learned those lessons and more while working in many other gardens, as both a gardener and a designer. I've continued to write for magazines and worked as a gardening editor and photographer, but it was as an instructor at the New York Botanical Garden that my philosophy of how to become a successful gardener developed. This led to the book you hold in your hands, where I share knowledge and advice harvested from my years of learning, doing, and teaching gardening.

Gardening is an intuitive art grounded in our understanding of a most basic and age-old pursuit. Gardening is also based on science. This book will encourage the intuitive gardener in you and help you learn the fundamental science of how plants grow and what they need in order to thrive. We start with the roots and the shoots—thinking about why we garden, your particular aims and dreams, and the basic botany of how plants work. From there we inquire into the living soil, the foundation upon which all gardens grow. Next comes plant selection, how to choose what to grow. The chapters that follow teach the hands-on gardening skills of starting plants from seeds, planting, mulching, watering, and feeding. Then, with a grasp of how to grow plants, we come to the advanced tasks of vegetative propagation and pruning. We end with the not-so-nice but unavoidable reality of dealing with weeds, pests, and diseases.

You can trust me to help you become a successful gardener. That's my goal in the classroom, and it's the purpose of this book. Gardeners grow by gardening, and to become a true gardener you must also learn to have fun in the garden. There is no fun in fretting, fussing, or worrying. Let your small successes build your confidence. Learn from your mistakes. It's a matter of entering the flow, forgetting your day-to-day cares, and linking your nature with *the* nature all around you. If you're ready for that, let's get started.

get
gardening

Balancing the
Roots and the Shoots

Plants lead relatively straightforward lives. They sprout, grow, and reproduce. Gardening teaches us how to participate in this life cycle, helping when we can and leaving well enough alone when we must.

Gardening is part faith in the future and part lessons from the past, but mostly it's the quality of our actions in the present that distinguish success from failure. The daily tasks, the doing, not the planning or reviewing, truly make a garden. Gardening is a live-in-the-moment activity with wonderful rewards reaped long after the hard work is done. Planting is an investment in the future—the garden's future, the gardener's future, and of course the future of the plants going into the ground.

Many people are drawn to gardening because they want to connect with nature, create beauty around their home, and/or grow food.

This investment in the future starts before we dig a hole. It starts when we decide to garden, when we choose to assume responsibility for living things and bring them home. Knowing why we want to garden, having a plot of land and a plan for it, having a few good tools, and knowing something about the living things we are going to populate our garden with are necessary first steps.

Why Garden?

I've taught hundreds of new gardeners how to garden, and the reasons they take my classes are varied yet predictable. The one goal they all share is a desire to connect with nature, to learn how to grow plants and interact successfully with the living environment. Other popular reasons my students want to garden are to create beauty around the home and to grow food.

Every gardener is unique, and it is from these primary aspirations that more general reasons to garden increase the motivation to grow. We want to enjoy the outdoors, relieve stress, spend time exercising or relaxing in fresh air and sunshine, express our creativity, or enjoy a sense of accomplishment. Those desires then lead to more specific objectives, such as growing show-quality cut flowers, building a plant collection, or creating habitat for pollinators and other wildlife.

New gardeners may start with a practical goal such as increasing the value of their home by surrounding it with healthy landscape plants, but in time they may find they have learned how to heal a damaged ecosystem through sustainable gardening practices or reduce energy use by providing shade and windbreaks for the house. Whatever the reason we get gardening, our focused engagement with plants and the land will shape our experiences as gardeners.

Select and Plan the Site

Many people start gardening out of necessity when they find themselves the owners of a plot of land surrounding their house. Others just want to garden and find that any bit of ground will do, even planters on a city terrace or pots on a fire escape. I gardened extensively—with permission—in the backyards of rented houses and apartments. Today I tend a small personal plot and mostly garden vicariously at client properties and by giving advice to students. Whatever your situation is, it's important to have a basic plan before you start planting.

When planning a garden, you can start with either the plants or the plot. I like to start with the site. Assess the sun, the soil, and the topography, and consider what you can grow under those conditions. Let's say, for example, that you want a vegetable garden. Most vegetables thrive in the sun, so if your backyard is filled with large trees and dense shade, either rethink what you will grow or alter conditions by editing the trees. But consider carefully. Are some tomatoes and peppers worth the destruction of a hundred-year-old oak tree? Maybe a woodland garden makes more sense. Soil, as you will learn later, can be improved, but slopes

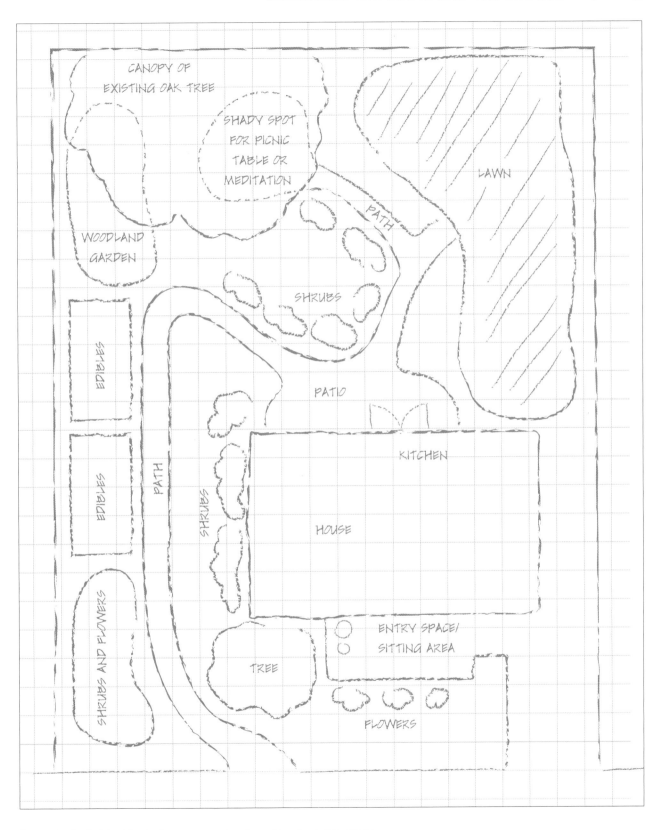

Draw a basic sketch of the features you want and roughly where they will be.

make a difference. Flat spaces are easy to plan and plant, while hillsides present problems but also opportunities for structures, like retaining walls and terraces. Low spots will collect water and, depending on the drainage, may offer the right conditions for water-loving plants.

Start by drawing a basic plan in pencil on graph paper. Situate the house within the property lines, then draw bubbles to divide the property into areas, or outdoor rooms, for different purposes, such as lawn to play on, edibles to eat, a patio to relax on, and ornamental beds with trees, shrubs, and flowers for visual appeal. Think about how you already use your yard, and which doors—back, front, or side—connect which interior rooms of the house to the outside. Consider convenience over artistry at this stage and let form follow function. You can tweak your plans for a more refined design later on.

If you choose to start with plants and let what you want to grow inform your planning decisions, be prepared for a bit more work and revisions to the site. It is understandable to have a list of "must have" plants. Many new gardeners are born from a passion for plants, and gardening isn't worth it if they can't grow what they want. My advice is to weigh the costs, for the gardener and the environment, when deciding to forego practical considerations to fulfill a dream.

There's a lot to think about when you plan a garden, but the basics of sun, soil, and topography will take you a long way. Gardening is, by nature, a dynamic process. Not even expert planners get everything right the first time. Experimentation is one of the many joys of gardening. Even when plants we wished for fail us, others take their place, and our developing passion to grow things takes root in that very special piece of ground we are working with.

Assemble the Right Tools

Acquiring and learning how to use the tools of the trade can be half the fun, just like for any other new hobby or pastime. I've twice set up shop at new garden estates where I was allowed to buy whatever I thought I needed. The first time, I was a relatively new gardener and bought several tools that proved unnecessary, such as a dibble. Others,

described here, became day-to-day mainstays as I learned which tools to carry with me whenever I went out to do some work in the garden.

Hand pruners Either holstered at your hip or tucked into a pocket, these are for those countless clips to roots and shoots as well as opening bags, trimming string, and cutting almost anything.

Sharp knife In lieu of hand pruners, a sharp knife is handy for cutting away packaging or dissecting plant parts.

Nursery trowel An eighteen-inch steel trowel with an elongated handle makes quick work when digging holes in compacted or prepared soil.

Stirrup or loop hoe This long-handled, hinged hoe is the most useful kind you can buy. Its dual-edge blade can be pulled back and forth to fluff mulch and soil while striking down weeds.

Burlap Also called hessian, it can be bought by the square or the roll and used as a mat when you are kneeling on bare dirt, to keep the lawn clean when dumping soil or mulch, to carry a root ball when transplanting, or to protect tender plants from unexpected frosts.

Bucket A five-gallon bucket gives you a place to store smaller tools and accessories, or can serve as a handy depository for weeds and clippings.

In later chapters of this book I describe the tools I have found essential for digging, watering, pruning, and weeding.

Getting tools and materials from place to place in the garden is easier with the right means of conveyance. Here are my recommendations:

Cart The best version is a four-foot-wide, five-foot-long, and three-foot-high open box riding atop an axle with two bicycle wheels and equipped with an aluminum handle.

Wheelbarrow Plastic barrows are lighter and easier to maneuver than metal but strong enough to hold loads of mulch, soil, and stone.

Trug This collapsible plastic bushel basket with handles is great for small loads or to fill with weeds.

Have a place where you can store your tools in an organized way.

Tarp Made of durable nylon, an eight-foot-square or larger tarp is a handy way to haul light materials like brush and leaves across a lawn to the compost pile.

Always buy top quality. You will save money in the long run with tools that last a lifetime instead of just a few seasons. Choose tools made from high-quality materials with excellent workmanship. Not only will they last longer, they will also work better. Avoid gimmicky tools with claims of making tasks quick and easy. Simple, traditional tools work perfectly well, though opting for lightweight materials is smart if they're sturdy. Over time you will collect an arsenal suited to your gardening needs and skills.

Keep your tools stored and organized so you can find them when you need them. A garden shed, a closet, or pegs on a wall work. Keep small hand tools in a bucket you can easily carry out to the garden. Hang up long-handled tools to save space or stack them in a wheelbarrow or garden cart. Never store tools outside. They will either rust, rot, or become lost. I spray paint a bright orange stripe on all my tool handles to help me find them after I set them down while working, a trick I learned after misplacing several expensive shovels and pairs of shears.

Always clean, sharpen, and oil your tools after each gardening session. Knives, pruners, and even spades and hoes work more effectively when they are sharpened after each use. Linseed oil is food and soil safe and can be used to lubricate metal tools and prevent them from rusting. After rinsing soil off with water, repeatedly dip spades and shovels into a bucket filled with sand and linseed oil. This will clean and coat the metal. Use rags to wipe off excess oil and/or sand before putting the tools away. The extra time and effort will keep your tools in top shape and ready at a moment's notice.

Learn How Plants Work

Good gardeners know how plants work, and the greatest gardens I have visited were designed and cared for by professional botanists or horticulturists. There's an old gardeners' adage I like to tell my students: "You don't know a plant until you've killed it three times." Well, I believe a firm grasp of basic botany can cut these losses by a third or better.

Botany provides a deeper understanding of plants, enabling us to visualize how they function inside and out. It's easy to perceive plants as static, but in fact they are always

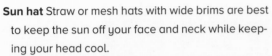

Tools for Personal Care and Safety

Your body is your most valuable tool, so taking care of yourself is as important as anything else you do out in the garden, requiring some care and precautions.

Sun hat Straw or mesh hats with wide brims are best to keep the sun off your face and neck while keeping your head cool.

Sun block Hours in the sun add up while gardening, so sun block designed to stay on when you sweat is crucial to protect your skin.

Bamboo cloth gloves with nitrile palms These gloves are the closest thing to gardening barehanded, allowing you to perform even the most delicate tasks. The cloth breathes well while the nitrile coating protects fingers and palms.

Goatskin gloves Leather gloves are best for tough work, like pruning woody plants or digging and raking. I prefer goatskin because it starts supple and stays that way.

Work boots Waterproof boots like wellies or muck boots are useful and popular, but any sturdy, medium-weight, ankle-high boot will work. Some people garden in sandals or rubber clogs, which are fine for light chores.

Bag balm Developed as a moisturizer for the udders of milking cows, this is the stuff farmers swear by to keep the skin on their hands from cracking.

Insect repellent Nothing shatters the patience of a gardener as quickly as the incessant assault of insects that swarm, bite, or sting. Find a repellent that works and use it.

Poison ivy soap For most of us who are allergic to poison ivies, sumacs, and oaks, the prospect of a painful, itchy rash makes washing up with this specialized soap after gardening a ritual of precaution.

Antihistamine The moment you notice your bare hand has plunged into that patch of poison ivy, or if a sting starts to swell, a timely dose of over-the-counter antihistamine can stop the reaction before it worsens. Always consult with your doctor, or other qualified health care professional, before using any new product or medication.

changing. They appear motionless but are always in motion because they are alive. Gardeners who recognize the movements of the inner life of plants and the flow of change that plants undergo, know plants better. Our actions join this flow and gardening intuition takes hold. That's when we become confident gardeners, because we intuitively know what to do.

For starters, it's important to understand that the plant we see is only half the story, even though it's usually what compels us to grow the plant. When we grow a plant we're responsible for all its parts, not just the pretty ones. The parts belowground (the roots) are crucial for plant health and just as much under our care as the top parts (the shoots). What grows below and above, the roots and the shoots, must be balanced for total plant health. Plants with vigorous stems, lots of leaves, pretty flowers, and tasty fruit require an equal measure of robust roots. The shoots return the favor, providing food and energy to grow and sustain the roots, creating a whole, healthy plant.

The gardener's first responsibility when caring for a plant is to provide the best possible conditions for strong roots and shoots. If you want beautiful roses, you must grow rose bushes with vigorous roots and strong stems. As a gardener, you can promote a balance between roots and shoots by providing proper sun exposure, good soil, sufficient water, and nutrients in the right measure. With that accomplished, you then can apply methods to control what and how the roots and the shoots produce.

What grows above and below, the shoots and the roots, must be balanced for total plant health.

Determinate and indeterminate growth

The roots and the shoots balance and support each other as a plant grows, but the growth of all plant parts can be divided into two categories: determinate and indeterminate.

The growth of leaves, flowers, fruits, and seeds is determinate. The size of these parts is primarily determined by genetics, though growing conditions are also a factor. Consider the leaves of a maple tree. In spring the leaves open and grow, but they don't keep growing throughout the season. They reach a certain size and then stop. That's determinate growth. The same is true of flowers. They open up to a certain size and that's it. Dinner plate dahlias are bred to make blooms as big as your head, while pompon dahlias grow to just an inch or two in diameter. Genetics also determines the potential of fruits and seeds, though their final size is influenced as well by the length of the growing season and the quality of the growing conditions.

Roots and stems grow indeterminately, meaning they have no fixed size. The roots of a plant start growing in the spring, and they keep growing. In temperate climates, winter halts this growth as the plants go dormant, but the following spring the roots start growing right where they left off in autumn. They keep adding on as long as there are nutrients, water, and oxygen available in the soil. When they encounter an underground obstacle, like the foundation of a building, a roadway, or a pond, they simply change direction and continue on.

The same is true for stems. It's obvious on woody trees and shrubs, as new growth starts from where it left off. However, the soft green stems of herbaceous plants that die back after a frost also grow indeterminately, but just for a single season. As long as the season lasts, they keep growing. Think lawns and wildflowers. In the case of plants genetically destined to live just one season, like corn or melons, their stems grow indeterminately throughout the season, and then the entire plant dies in the fall, roots and all.

The aim of every gardener, and the key to successful gardening, is to promote indeterminate growth and control determinate growth. Gardeners promote indeterminate growth by providing the best possible growing conditions for their plants. When we know what a particular plant needs in order to thrive and we provide it, the plant will respond by growing strong roots and shoots. Gardeners control determinate growth through interactions with the plant itself, such as pruning and feeding. By harnessing the energy within a plant, as evidenced by the vitality of its indeterminate parts, the gardener can make a plant bloom bigger and brighter or produce higher-quality fruits.

▲ Roots and stems have no fixed size.

◄ Leaves, flowers, fruits, and seeds grow to a predetermined, fixed size.

How plants grow

How, exactly, do roots and stems grow? The primary growth process of all living things is cell division, or mitosis. Cell division takes place within the specialized growth tissue of a plant, called meristematic tissue or meristem. Primary growth occurs in the apical meristem, located at the tip of a root or stem. In addition, plants have axillary meristem in discrete spots along the length of their roots and stems, where branching or budding can occur. Growth tissue distributed along the entire length of each root or stem is called lateral meristem. It contributes to the thickening of the root or stem to provide strength and support, turning twigs into branches and branches into boughs.

Gardener's Glossary

All plants either develop woody stems or stay herbaceous, with pliable stems. Trees and shrubs produce herbaceous shoots in the spring that transform into woody stems. Woody plants are also perennials, which means they live more than two years, sometimes for centuries. Herbaceous plants don't form woody stems but can be annuals, biennials, or tender or hardy perennials.

Annuals are single-season plants that are genetically programmed to germinate, grow, flower, fruit, and die in a single season, sometimes sooner. Many crop plants and common weeds are annuals.

Biennials are plants that require two years to reach maturity. The first year they germinate and grow, making plenty of stems and leaves but no flowers, fruit, or seeds. Come winter they die down to the ground, but the roots survive so they can spring up again next season. During the second year, biennials make flowers and set seed. Thereafter the plant dies and disappears, its only vestiges some random seedlings that pop up nearby the following spring.

Tender perennials are genetic perennials but last only one year when grown in climates with winters that get too cold for them. These include many fast-growing flowers typically planted in beds for temporary seasonal displays (known as bedding plants), like impatiens, petunias, geraniums, and marigolds. The closer you live to the equator, the more likely these plants will be to last more than one season in your garden.

Hardy perennials come back year after year. Their tops may die back during the winter, but their roots remain alive so they resprout in the spring. Perennials can be woody, semiwoody, or herbaceous.

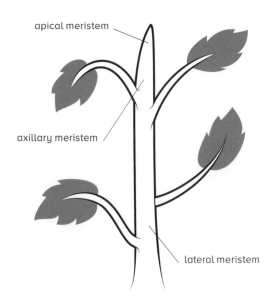

apical meristem

axillary meristem

lateral meristem

Growth points along a stem where cell division takes place are known as meristematic tissue or meristem.

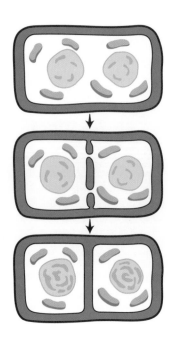

Plants grow by cell division (mitosis) that takes place in the meristem.

Mitosis requires sun energy, water, and nutrients to fuel cell division. In the absence of adequate sunlight, a measure that varies from plant to plant, plants resort to another growth process called elongation. Cell walls swell with water, soften, and expand. The threads of cellulose within the cell wall loosen and spread so that the cells bulge on two sides. When the pressure is relieved, the cells slim back and elongate lengthwise.

Cell elongation results in leggy plants with weak stems and explains why plants on a windowsill reach toward the sun. The meristematic tissue exposed to sunlight has enough energy for mitosis, resulting in regular-size, sturdy cells. Meristem with insufficient sun exposure doesn't have enough energy to divide, so the cells resort to elongation and that side of the stem grows longer than the other, causing the stem to bend toward the sunlight.

Anatomy of a plant cell

Plant cells are similar to the cells in our bodies but with two important differences. First, while animal cells have membranes only, plant cells have membranes and walls.

Made of cellulose, a rigid, lightweight material, cell walls support the plant, similar to how our skeletons support us. Attached to the inside of the wall is a cell membrane that controls what passes in and out of the cell. Inside the membrane is a jellylike material called cytoplasm. Floating in the cytoplasm are specialized parts, the organelles. A second difference between plant and animal cells is that plant cells have an organelle called a chloroplast.

Chloroplasts contain chlorophyll, the magic ingredient that makes photosynthesis work, enabling plants to convert sunlight into energy. Plant cells and animal cells alike

To help indoor plants grow strong and straight, give them a quarter turn each week to provide consistent sun exposure on all sides. Half turns are no good. The plant will flop back and forth, resulting in a weakened form.

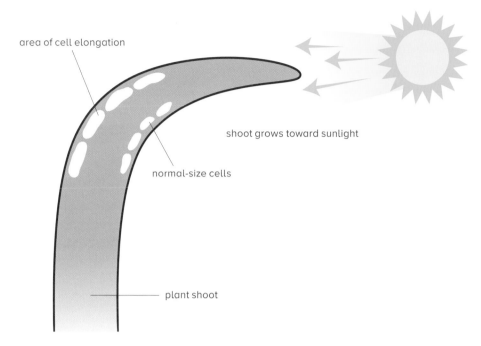

area of cell elongation

shoot grows toward sunlight

normal-size cells

plant shoot

Plants grown without enough sunlight will elongate, resulting in leggy plants with weak stems.

contain sausage-shaped mitochondria, organelles that also produce energy for the cell. Each cell has a nucleus, the brain of the cell, where the genetic code of the plant or animal is stored.

As gardeners we don't have direct influence over how cell parts function, but there is one feature in a plant cell that we can affect: the vacuole. The vacuole, as the name suggests, is an empty compartment within the cell. It is used to store extra water and nutrients for plant metabolism. By watering and fertilizing, gardeners help plants fill their vacuoles with reserves the cells can use when the source of water or nutrients is interrupted, such as during a drought or in depleted soil. Vacuoles are also where cells stash potentially harmful substances absorbed from contaminated soil, segregating these toxins from the cytoplasm.

The water held in the vacuole exerts pressure on the cytoplasm, which transfers pressure to the cell walls. This pressure keeps the cell structure stiff. If the water inside the vacuole is depleted and pressure is lost, the cell walls collapse and the plant wilts. Some plants work around this kind of collapse by developing woody stems. Their cell walls form secondary walls made of a material called

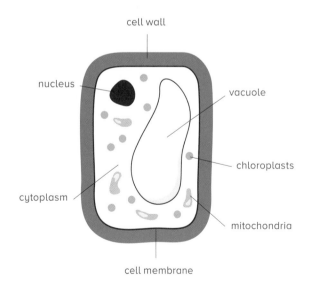

cell wall

nucleus

vacuole

chloroplasts

cytoplasm

mitochondria

cell membrane

A plant cell has walls and chloroplasts, two features that animal cells lack. It also has a very large vacuole to store extra water and nutrients.

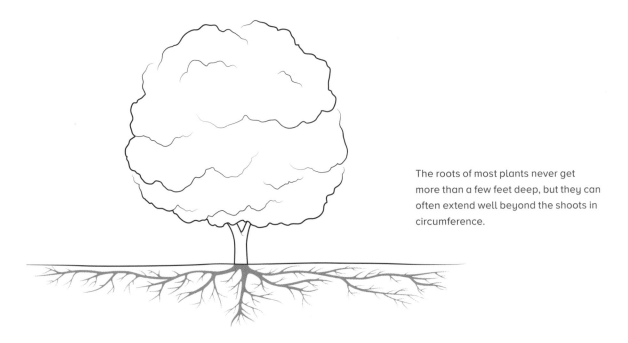

The roots of most plants never get more than a few feet deep, but they can often extend well beyond the shoots in circumference.

lignin, a hardening substance that is durable enough to support the plant.

Root functions and growth

An early misconception when someone is learning about plants is that the roots belowground look just like the branches above. I too believed that was how plants grew, but I was wrong. The parts of a plant growing aboveground look very different from the parts of a plant growing below-ground. In fact, while the shoots of a plant may grow more than a hundred feet tall, the roots of most plants never get much deeper than just a few feet. Roots don't always grow deep, but they often range far distances from their shoots. The roots of a large shade tree, for example, extend well beyond its canopy.

Roots seem mysterious because we see them only when planting, but their health can be inferred from the vigor of aboveground parts. Many symptoms of a plant in poor health, such as yellowing of leaves or wilting, can be traced back to the condition of its roots.

Roots link the aerial parts of plants to the earth and support the shoots in every way. They perform four functions:

Anchor the plant to the soil. Roots quite literally keep a plant from tipping over, and on spreading species they attach to the ground, keeping the plant in place on steep slopes.

Absorb water. All the water a plant needs is absorbed from the soil. Spritzing a plant is nice and helps cool and clean the leaves, but the water required to keep a plant alive comes from the ground through the roots.

Acquire mineral nutrients. Plants get the vast majority of key nutrients from the soil. Roots grow into fertile ground where they find the ingredients needed to build all plant tissue.

Store food. Roots store food for themselves and for us. In the case of a carrot, we harvest and eat it. Perennial plants use the energy from sugars stored in their roots to help sprout anew each spring.

There are two types of roots: fibrous and tap. Fibrous roots are less fleshy than taproots, with less food storage but much greater surface area. More surface area means more water absorbed from the soil. Fibrous roots acquire nutrients more effectively from a given volume of soil, and their dense web of growth limits soil erosion by clinging to soil particles.

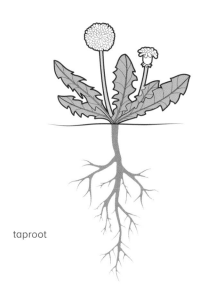

taproot

fibrous root

Roots can be either fibrous or taproots.

Taproots are great anchors that grow deep into the ground, and their large food storage capacity allows them to regenerate. If you pull a dandelion and don't get the whole root, expect the weed to grow back. Conifers are an exception. They have deep taproots but do not regenerate from them because their taproots don't store a lot of food. Conifers store food in their needles.

Taproots can go to great depths in search of water and nutrients, so plants with taproots tend to tolerate harsh growing conditions, such as frequent drought or infertile soils. Many native plants that fend for themselves in the wild have well-developed taproots, while cultivated varieties raised in gardens are bred for fibrous roots. Easier to grow in containers or transplant from the field, plants with fibrous roots are preferred among nursery growers over taproot plants that are difficult to dig with their roots intact.

Some plants, such as oak trees, have a combination of the two. They start with taproots but also develop a network of fibrous roots close to the surface. This provides the best of both types but also the limitations. It's a good idea to know the kinds of roots you're working with, especially when digging and also when determining the water and nutrient needs of the plants you're going to grow. Find out

if the roots are fibrous, tap, or both by examining the root structure directly before planting or looking up the plant's "root morphology."

Root growth is indeterminate, slow and persistent. Each year new roots are added to what grew before. Hence the popular saying among gardeners about herbaceous perennials: "The first year they sleep, the second year they creep, and the third year they leap." As the roots get bigger, the shoots follow suit.

Cells produced by apical meristems extend the root tips in search of water and minerals. The apical root meristem is covered by a root cap. Conditions belowground are not particularly friendly, and meristems pushing through dirt and rocks can easily be damaged. If meristematic tissue is damaged it dies, so the root cap protects the tip as it pushes through the soil. The roots continue to grow in any direction where water and minerals are available. When there's none, the root either alters course or stops growing.

Lateral roots develop to explore more soil around the base of the plant. The root system expands as roots branch off where axillary meristem develops into new apical meristem, complete with a root cap. Surface area is increased by root hairs that grow on new lateral roots and root tips.

These delicate extensions develop from the outermost cells of root "skin." If damaged, they won't heal. The plant will make more someplace else, but this saps its strength.

Shoots and plant metabolism

Balancing the roots, the shoots (stems and leaves) grow aboveground and out in the open, uninhibited by obstacles. The shape, size, and color of the shoots may vary, but they all share one basic rule of growth: laying claim bit by bit to a little more of the world. For trees, the shoot system has three main parts: the trunk, the branches, and the leaves. The purpose of the shoot structure is to expose as many leaves—harvesters of the light—to as much sun as possible, to power the plant's metabolism.

Plant metabolism consists of four fundamental activities, all of which are required for life and growth. Two, respiration and transpiration, are in common with humans. The other two, photosynthesis and assimilation, are wholly unique to plants, making them remarkable contributors to the ultimate survival of all life on earth.

Photosynthesis is the conversion of solar energy, carbon dioxide, and water in the presence of chlorophyll (in chloroplasts) into oxygen and sugars.

Respiration is the process whereby plants burn these sugars (in mitochondria) in the presence of oxygen to build living cells, releasing carbon dioxide and water as by-products.

Transpiration is plant perspiration, the release of water in gaseous form from its leaves. When a plant is actively growing, it uses water absorbed from the soil. The majority of this water, however, passes through the plant and is released from microscopic pores in the leaves, cooling the plant and providing transport of minerals from the roots to the shoots.

The purpose of a tree's shoot structure is to expose leaves to sunlight.

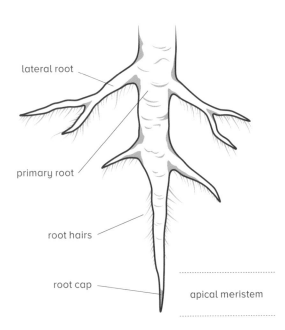

lateral root

primary root

root hairs

root cap

apical meristem

Roots grow as cells produced by the apical meristem extend the root tips in search of water and minerals.

Assimilation is a plant's formation of living protoplasm from nonliving elements. In the same way that people eat food and assimilate it through digestion to make the building blocks for our living cells, plants assimilate mineral nutrients to create life. Plant assimilation is why plants are essential for all life on earth. Animals can't eat dirt and absorb sunlight to make living tissue. Plants can. Humans must eat living things in order to live: plants directly, or other animals that eat plants.

Stem structure and growth

Stem growth is indeterminate, just like root growth. If a plant is alive, its stems continue to grow. This growth may be interrupted by winter, but for perennial plants growth will start anew the following spring. The rate of shoot growth does fluctuate from season to season, limited by the supply of water, nutrients, and sunlight. Tree rings of different thicknesses are a testament to this.

The terminal (or apical) bud at the end of a stem is the growth point where cell division takes place, extending the tip of the branch farther away from the principal stem, or trunk. Axillary buds are arranged in discrete spots along the length of the stem. This meristematic tissue can develop into a few things: a flower, a leaf, or a new branch. Some become flowers, then leaves. Others just become leaves, but a few will form a branch to enlarge the shoot system.

During photosynthesis, plants convert solar energy, carbon dioxide, and water into oxygen and sugars. During respiration, plants burn sugars to build living cells, giving off carbon dioxide and water.

During transpiration, plants release water in gaseous form from pores in their leaves.

Axillary buds are located at nodes. Even when the buds are small or dormant, you can find a node on a stem by the slight bulge often marked with a thin circumferential line. The space between nodes is called an internode. Internodes can be short or long. Slow-growing plants with dense branching, like boxwood and rosemary, have short internodes. Fast, loose growers, like bridal wreath or oleander, have long internodes.

Leaf structure and function

Most plants have both stems and leaves. Some plants, like cacti, have no leaves, only stems, while some other plants, like grasses, have no stems, only leaves. Yes, the needles on a pine tree are leaves. Many plants are grown solely for their leaves, like lettuce to eat or an elm tree for shade. Even if a plant is grown for its flowers and fruit, like peonies and tomatoes, its leaves power the production of these parts. The primary purpose of all leaves is photosynthesis, and every leaf is perfectly designed to gather sunlight and convert it into food to fuel the plant.

A simple design technique is to vary leaf sizes and shapes when combining ornamental plants in the garden. This adds interest through textural contrast.

The vast majority of leaves are determinate growers. They start small, reach a certain size, and then stop growing. This means leaves, unlike stems and roots, don't heal. If a leaf is damaged, it won't repair itself, though if it's removed, the plant can grow a new one. Most leaves have the basic

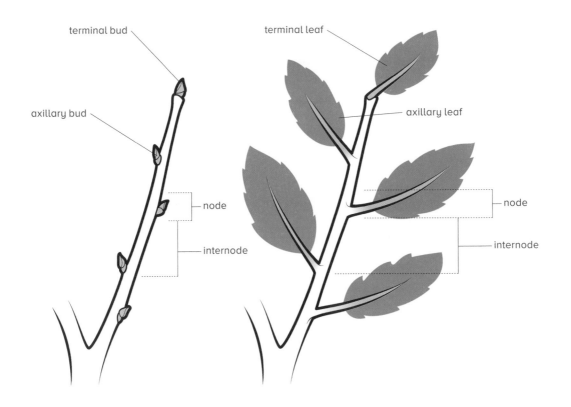

Stems grow longer when cells in the terminal bud divide. Axillary buds can develop into flowers, leaves, or branches.

The Vascular System: Xylem Up, Phloem Down and Around

The stem of a plant is central to its vascular system, which is analogous to the circulatory system that carries blood throughout our bodies. The vascular system moves water, minerals, and food between the roots and the shoots and throughout the plant. Xylem (Greek for "wood"), located toward the center of the stem, carries mineral nutrients and water absorbed by the roots up to the shoots. Phloem (Greek for "bark") carries sugars, a product of photosynthesis, from the leaves throughout the plant and down to the roots. This flow strikes a balance between the roots and the shoots as each provides for the other.

Injury to either the xylem or the phloem can have disastrous effects on the vigor of a plant. Phloem, positioned beneath the bark of a tree, is often damaged by lawn equipment. Repeated, careless use of a string trimmer around the base of a tree can pierce the bark and cut the phloem, stopping the supply of sugars from the leaves to the roots. The result is a slow, unseen decline of the roots, symptoms of which won't be noticed for a year or more, when the top parts of the tree begin to suffer.

Phloem is often damaged by lawn equipment, stopping the supply of food from the leaves to the roots.

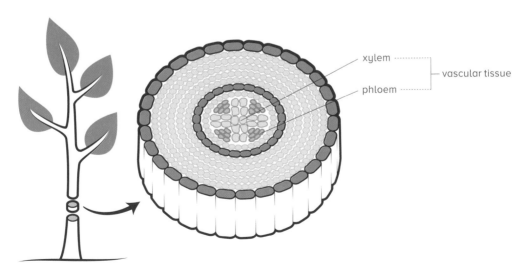

Vascular tissue in the roots and shoots consists of xylem and phloem.

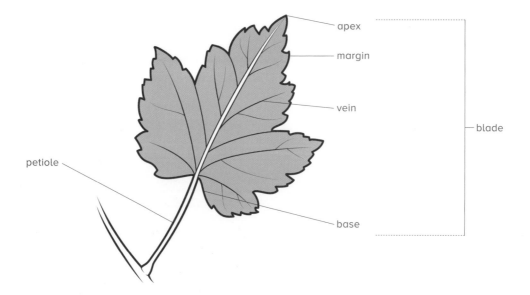

Most leaves have the basic form of a petiole and a blade.

form of a petiole (the little stalk attaching the leaf to the stem) and a blade. Each blade has four distinct features: apex, margin, vein, and base. These features vary from plant to plant and combine to form an identifiable shape.

Leaves possess one key feature all gardeners should know about: stomata. Stomata are microscopic openings on leaves that facilitate gas exchange and water release. On most plants these pores are on the underside of the leaf, keeping them free from dust and debris. However, the stomata on water plants, such as lotus, are located on the top of the leaf. Plants with vertical leaves, like grasses, tend to have stomata on both top and underside. The number of stomata affects plant transpiration, hence the rate at which water passes from the soil through the vascular system and out to the atmosphere. The transpiration rates of our plants impact how often we water them.

Each stoma allows gases to enter and exit the leaf. Carbon dioxide, required for photosynthesis, comes in, and oxygen and water vapor, products of photosynthesis, go out. Two guard cells border each opening. When water is present, the guard cells swell, causing them to bend so the pore opens. When dry, the guard cells lie straight, keeping the pore closed. Typically closed at night and open during the day, stomata respond to environmental conditions and plant metabolism.

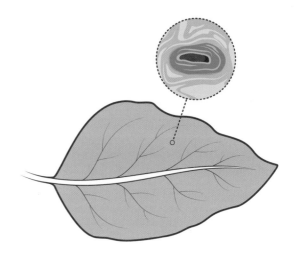

Stomata are microscopic pores in leaves through which plants breathe.

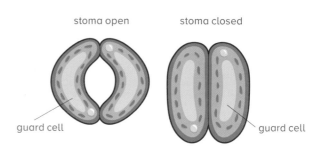

Stomata open when water is present and close when dry.

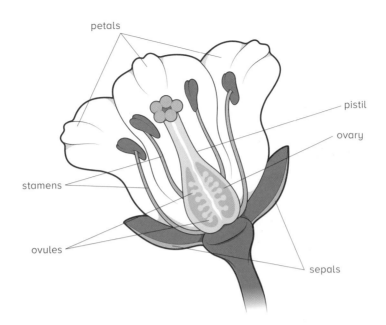

petals

pistil

ovary

stamens

ovules

sepals

Every gardener should be able to speak intelligently about flower parts.

Flower parts and function

When a plant reaches maturity and has sufficient sunlight, nutrients, and water, some of the axillary buds on a stem develop into flowers. The parts of a flower are simple to understand: the petals are pretty, and the rest perform functions related to reproduction. Every gardener should be able to speak intelligently about a flower, for a rose by any other name is just a collection of petals, stamens, a pistil, ovules, and sepals. Such terminology might dull their romantic charm, but I believe a measure of botanical appreciation is requisite for a true love of flowers.

Petals come in countless colors, shapes, and sizes and are why many people want to grow plants. Petals serve a practical purpose: to attract insects that will ideally transfer some pollen from a stamen to a pistil.

Stamens are the male parts of a flower that carry the pollen that fertilizes the flower. Most flowers have several.

The **pistil** is the female part of a flower. It receives the pollen and conducts it to the ovary, which grows into a fruit with seeds.

Ovules are eggs, but when we're talking about plants we mean seeds. Seeds form inside the ovary only when it has been pollinated and develops into a fruit. After the flower finishes, the seeds in the ovary ripen and are disseminated to make more plants.

Sepals are those little green leaves at the base of the flower. They protect the delicate structure of the flower during the bud stage before it opens. Sometimes sepals are very small, like on blueberries, but sometimes they're quite large, as on flag irises, where they are often larger than the petals.

Most flowers have both male and female parts, but some have only female parts and some have only male parts. If a plant has both male and female flowers, or flowers with both male and female parts, it is termed monoecious and can pollinate itself and others of the same genus. Most plants are monoecious. If a plant has only male flowers or only female flowers, it is known as dioecious and requires a different plant of the same genus but the opposite sex nearby to complete pollination. Pollinators such as bees and butterflies can help by carrying pollen from flower to flower and plant to plant.

The red parts of a pointsettia are not petals; they are modified leaves surrounding the little yellow flowers in the center.

Common Monoecious Plants	Common Dioecious Plants
TREES	**TREES**
alder	ash
birch	aspen
cypress	holly
fir	juniper
pine	mulberry
spruce	persimmon
walnut	willow
EDIBLES	**EDIBLES**
beans	asparagus
cucumbers	kiwi fruit
melons	spinach
peas	
peppers	
pumpkins	
squash	
tomatoes	

Once pollinated, flowers turn into fruit. The petals fade and fall off as the ovary swells, though the sepals often persist at the base of the fruit attached to the stem. The lesson here is: no flowers = no fruit. Fruit contains seeds, the end game for a flower, but the seeds aren't ready right away. For seeds to propagate, they must ripen. Then the ovary will open and release them.

All this botany is a lot for the new gardener to absorb, but the most important takeaway is this: gardeners are responsible for what goes on beneath the earth's surface as much as for what happens above it. If we want to balance the roots and the shoots, we must attend to the environment where the roots live. That's the soil, topic of the next chapter.

Symbolism and human passions aside, flowers exist exclusively to perform reproduction. Flowers turn into fruit as the ovary swells, and seeds ripen inside.

soil

Nourishing the Roots

Soil is the foundation upon which all gardens grow, so a gardener's first goal is to make healthy soil. Without success in this, you will never grow healthy plants. But what is soil? The best description I ever read comes from Ralph Snodsmith, beloved gardening instructor and creator of the Fundamentals of Gardening course at the New York Botanical Garden. In his lecture notes I found the following sentence: "Soil is a living and dynamic system that is fragile and perishable." It changed the way I think about soil—the soil in gardens, in farm fields, in meadows or forests. These words also inform how I teach what it means to make healthy soil as a gardener.

Soil is alive. All good garden soil teems with life: billions of microbes and fungi and countless insects and worms. Our soil is not inanimate. *Soil is dynamic.* The soil in a garden is always changing. Day to day, month to month, year to year, fertility rises and falls, water comes and goes, and organic matter is born, lives, and dies. It's a perpetual cycle all gardeners participate in. Our soil is not static. *Soil is fragile.* We can wreck a soil's structure by physically compacting it with work trucks or repeated footsteps. We can break our soil. Finally, *soil is perishable.* If it's alive, it can die. Spill a little gasoline by mistake or apply synthetic fertilizers, herbicides, or pesticides, and the living ingredients in the soil suffer. We can kill our soil.

The common truth is that unless you've been growing organically, your soil is likely junk, especially beneath a traditional lawn propped up with chemicals. So you first must make healthy soil that is structurally sound, holds water well, and is fertile, understanding that good garden soil is alive, dynamic, fragile, and perishable. In this chapter, as you learn how to evaluate and improve your soil, you will realize that what you know about soil may be the most important gardening instruction you ever receive. Soil truly is the fundamental source of life for everything we grow.

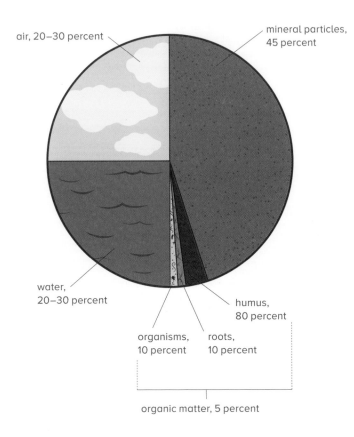

Soil is composed of mineral particles, air, water, and organic matter in percentages that change over time.

What Makes Up Soil?

Soil has four constant ingredients: mineral particles, air, water, and organic matter. The percentages of each that make up the whole change over time. Organic matter, the living ingredient, is further divided into three categories: the roots of the plants growing in the soil, the organisms of the soil food web, and humus.

A soil is said to have good tilth when it holds water without becoming soggy, allows air to penetrate, and is loose and easy to work. This occurs when there's a proper balance among the percentages of air, water, minerals, and organic matter—roughly 25 percent air, 25 percent water, 45 percent minerals, and 5 percent organic matter. Soil with a mineral volume of 60 percent or higher and correspondingly low volumes of water and air is considered structurally compacted. Compacted soil is difficult to

garden in because the roots have trouble pushing through and less water and air are available for plant metabolism. Unlike physical compaction caused by car tires or too many footsteps, structural compaction can't be solved by tilling the soil. The only way to fix it is by increasing the organic matter.

This means adding humus or compost, and that's where many home gardeners go wrong. Somewhere along the way we've been told to "clean up" the garden each fall—to rake out the beds, or worse yet, send in backpack blowers. Nothing could be worse for the soil. No one blows the leaves out of the forest, yet the trees survive. No one rakes a wild meadow, but the plants return each year. In nature, the organic material that falls to the ground decomposes on the ground, feeding the soil food web and by extension the plants.

Humus in a soil is depleted as it improves tilth and fuels the growth of plants and organisms. We are tasked to replenish the organic matter in our soils, either passively by allowing the detritus that falls on the ground to naturally break down or actively by spreading a layer of compost on the ground an inch or two deep. In fact, as you will learn throughout this chapter, adding organic matter is the answer to most soil issues. I tell my students: "When in doubt, use OM, short for organic matter, as your soil improvement mantra. For example: 'How can I fix my soil? OOOMMM!' 'What's the most important ingredient in my soil? OOOOMMMM!'"

Regional Soil Types

Every region has its own soil type, which directly impacts the kinds of plants that grow there. While soil quality does differ from garden to garden as a result of how it's been cultivated, the soil we start with has been forming for decades, centuries, or even millennia. This formation is driven by three key factors: climate, topography, and geology.

Climate is determined by the temperature and rainfall prevailing in an area over a long period of time. For example, a subtropical climate has hot, humid summers and mild winters; a Mediterranean climate has hot, dry summers and mild, moist winters. The difference between plants grown in a woodland garden and in a desert garden is the result of climate conditions and the soil formed under those conditions. Each climate's plant life reinforces the formation of the existing soil type by contributing unique organic material as detritus.

Topography is the shape, height, and depth of a land surface, which affects soil formation on local and regional scales in the form of erosion and deposits. Consider land in a fertile valley. As the hillsides erode, rich deposits collect below. A similar result can be seen in a small garden plot where better topsoil is found in a low spot compared to an adjacent slope.

Geology is the rock base, the parent material that is the primary source of the mineral elements of a soil, the size and type of which determine soil texture, pH, and nutrient composition. For example, the parent material for many soils in the northeastern United States is granite, hence coarsely textured; in Dover, England, it's limestone, making the soil highly alkaline; and on an island in the Pacific, it's volcanic and thus porous and fertile.

Gardener's Glossary

Tilth is what soil is said to have when it holds water without becoming soggy, allows air to penetrate, and is loose and easy to work.

The **soil food web** is the symbiotic population of microbes, insects, worms, and fungi living in healthy soil.

Organic matter is any plant or animal material, dead or alive, present in the soil, either naturally occurring or added by the gardener.

Humus is organic matter decomposed naturally by the soil food web in the soil of a garden, farm, or natural setting.

Compost is organic matter biodegraded purposely by a gardener who provides adequate amounts of nitrogen- and carbon-rich ingredients, air, water, warmth, and microbes.

Amendments are natural ingredients added to a soil to improve its structure, fertility, and water-holding ability or to adjust soil acidity.

Top-dressing is the placement of amendments on the surface of the soil, allowing them to infiltrate over time rather than working them physically into the ground. **Topdressing** is also the term for the amendments you top-dress with.

Mulch is any material, organic or nonorganic, spread on the ground to mitigate environmental impacts on the soil and plants.

The Soil Food Web

The soil food web is why we say soil is alive. It starts with the sun, which provides energy for plants to grow as photosynthesis converts sunlight into sugars. This fuels plant metabolism to make roots and shoots. Some plants grow for years, others just a season, but they all deposit organic matter on the ground.

This detritus is the first link in the soil food web. As food for fungi and bacteria, detritus decomposes. The microbes are then eaten by tiny bugs and worms, which are food for bigger bugs and worms, all adding layers of life to the soil.

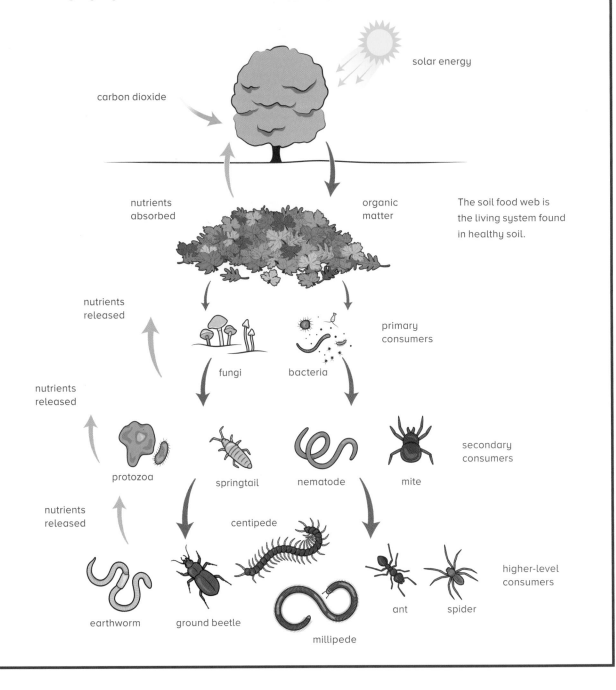

solar energy

carbon dioxide

nutrients absorbed

organic matter

The soil food web is the living system found in healthy soil.

nutrients released

fungi

bacteria

primary consumers

nutrients released

protozoa

springtail

nematode

mite

secondary consumers

nutrients released

centipede

earthworm

ground beetle

millipede

ant

spider

higher-level consumers

Soil Texture: Clay, Silt, Sand, Loam

The mineral portion of the soil consists of particles of different sizes. Soil texture is determined by the proportion of different particle sizes, as represented in the soil texture triangle. What's important to note is that any extreme in soil texture makes it difficult to grow most plants effectively. I've gardened in soil textures from several regions, including fertile river terrace loam, fast-draining island sand, heavy piedmont clay, and rock-filled glacial deposits. I struggled and succeeded in each and learned that every soil poses distinct challenges but also offers unique advantages.

A sand particle is huge compared to a clay particle, and silt is sized closer to clay. Since sand and clay are so distinct, we tend to focus on them while giving silt short shrift. We hope against soil that is predominantly of one particle size, such as all sand or a lot of clay. The best soil has a balance of particle sizes. This is the sweet spot in the lower center of the soil texture triangle where soil is 40 percent sand particles, 40 percent silt particles, and 20 percent clay particles. That's loam, and loam is what we want for most garden plants. In fact, any soil texture described with the word *loam* will do—clay loam, silt loam, sandy loam, they're all good.

Soil texture affects how we garden, but trying to change your soil's texture is not practical. The volume of material is just too large, on the order of hundreds of cubic yards for even a small plot. Growing in pots or planters is different, because that's soil we make and put in place. On garden ground what can be improved is soil structure, the arrangement of soil particles into groupings called aggregates.

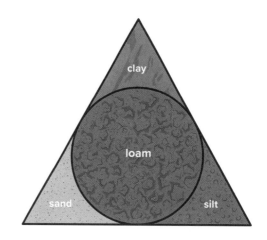

Soil texture is determined by the mix of particle sizes in the mineral ingredients, as shown in the soil texture triangle.

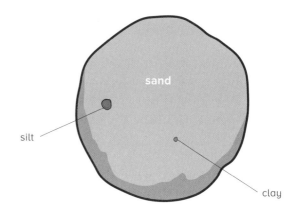

Sand particles are huge compared to silt and clay particles.

An At-Home Soil Texture Test

Assess your soil's texture by performing this simple field test:

1. Pick up a clump of soil and get it a little wet with water.
2. Squeeze the soil in your hand.
3. Open your hand. If the clump crumbles, you have sandy soil.
4. If the clump holds together, poke it. If it crumbles, you have loam.
5. If you poke the clump and it holds firm, it's clay soil.

Test your soil texture by moistening and squeezing.

What Organic Matter Does for Your Soil

Humus or compost, it makes no difference, is always the first prescription for solving soil problems. It sounds easy to say—"Add humus. Add compost"—but to improve soil, it's the right thing to do every time. Adding organic matter improves your soil's structure, water-holding capacity, and fertility.

Improves your soil's structure

When we add organic matter to a soil, in the form of compost or humus, it coats the particles of sand, silt, or clay and they clump together, forming aggregates. Aggregates of soil particles are like marbles in a jar. Piled on top of each other, they leave space for air, water, and plant roots. The result is improved soil structure, or good tilth.

Improves your soil's water-holding capacity

All the water plants use for metabolism is held in the soil. A soil's capacity for water retention, called its field capacity, is enhanced by adding organic matter. Since humus improves soil structure by forming aggregates that enlarge the pore spaces, more water can infiltrate. Also, the humus forms a film around the aggregates, holding water in place as if the soil were a sponge.

When it's raining, water fills the pores between soil particles and the soil becomes saturated. There's no room for oxygen in the soil, and the roots of most plants can't

Gardener's Glossary

Soil texture is a quality determined by the relative proportions or varied sizes of particles of sand, silt, and clay in a soil.

Soil structure is the arrangement of soil particles into aggregates of different sizes and shapes and the pore spaces created by this arrangement.

Field capacity is the maximum amount of water held in a soil after the excess is drawn away by gravity.

Soil pH is a measure of the acidity and/or alkalinity of a soil.

Nutrients are the chemical building blocks, mineral and nonmineral, essential for plant health and growth.

Soil fertility is the potential for a soil to provide nutrients necessary for plant growth, determined by a scientific measurement called cation exchange capacity.

respire (notable exceptions include water lovers like mangroves, cattails, and lotus), so metabolism stops. When the rain ends, gravity pulls most of the water down to the bedrock, leaving only what the soil can hold. This is the water plants use. Soils with high field capacity hold a lot of water for the plants to use. If field capacity is poor, less water is available, the soil dries out quickly, and the plants wilt. Wilting is bad for plants because it damages cell walls, sometimes permanently.

Garden soils with low field capacity, like the sandy soil I worked on a coastal island in North Carolina, need frequent watering, even when it rains. If the soil can't hold on to the water, it doesn't matter how much it rains today. Most of it will drain away and the garden will need to be watered tomorrow. Plants growing in soil with good field capacity, like the loam I found along a Mississippi River terrace, do fine with less frequent watering because ample moisture is retained between rain events. Plants growing in heavy, slow-draining clay like I encountered on the Georgia piedmont are in danger of becoming waterlogged. When the right amount of water is always available, plants (and gardeners) avoid stress and thrive.

dispersed state

humus gluing the mineral particles together

aggregated state

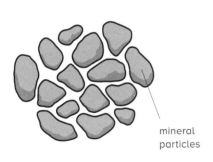

mineral particles

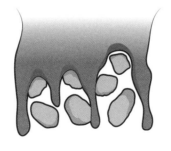

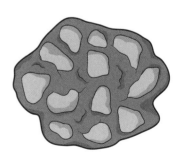

Adding humus causes soil particles to aggregate, leaving space for air, water, and plant roots.

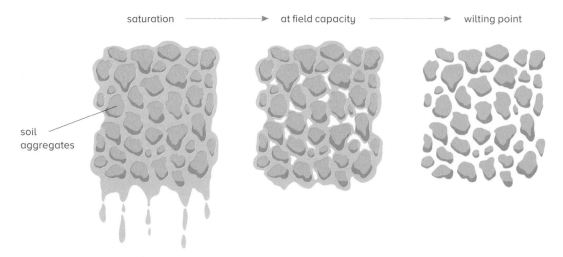

saturation ⟶ at field capacity ⟶ wilting point

soil aggregates

The field capacity of a soil is how much water it can retain after being saturated. The greater the field capacity, the longer plants can last before reaching the wilting point.

Improves your soil's fertility

Plants gather nutrients through underground chemical reactions called cation (pronounced *cat-ion*) exchanges. Basically, cations are swapped between plant roots and soil particles. Mineral nutrients attach to clay and humus in the soil. As plant roots spread through the soil, they encounter these nutrients clinging to bits of humus and clay. The plant absorbs the nutrients and uses them to grow.

Soil is considered fertile when capable of exchanging lots of nutrients with plant roots. The higher the humus and clay content of a soil is, the greater is its cation exchange capacity and thus fertility. Because the clay content is relatively constant, the only way gardeners can increase fertility is by adding organic matter, typically in the form of compost. OM!

Soil pH and Nutrient Availability

Soil pH is a measure of the acidity or alkalinity of your soil. The lower the number, the higher the acidity, and because the pH scale is logarithmic, soil with a pH of 5 is ten times more acidic than soil with a pH of 6, and a hundred times more acidic than a soil with a pH of 7. The pH range suitable for plants is 4.5 to 7.8, and the majority of garden soils fall well within the optimal range of 5 to 7.

The pH of a soil matters because it determines nutrient availability. For example, at a pH of 4 practically no nitrogen, phosphorus, or potassium, the key nutrients for plant growth, will swap from a clay or humus particle to a root. As we move up the pH scale more nutrients can make the exchange, though even at a pH of 6, phosphorus is still reluctant to switch. Plants have pH preferences based on the nutrients they need. The next chapter goes into more detail about this.

A fun way to discover the approximate acidity of your soil is to plant a blue-flowering hydrangea. Hydrangea flowers bloom blue year after year when grown in acid (sometimes called sour) soil, but they gradually turn pink after several seasons if the soil is alkaline (often referred to as sweet).

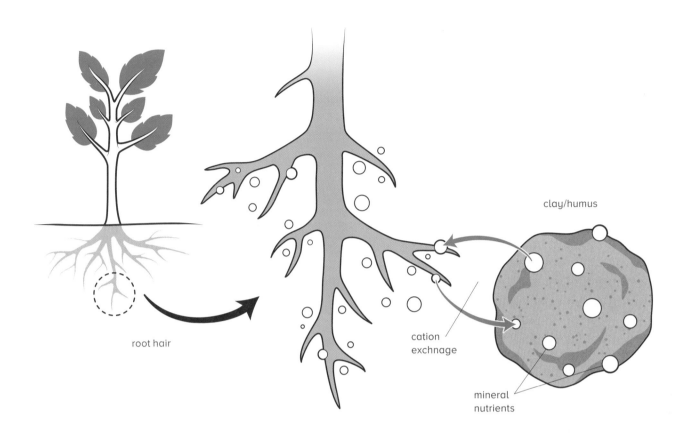

root hair

clay/humus

cation exchnage

mineral nutrients

Plant roots absorb minerals attached to bits of humus and clay in the soil, so adding humus increases soil fertility.

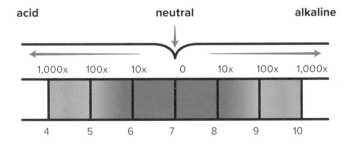

The soil pH scale measures the acidity or alkalinity of the soil and is logarithmic.

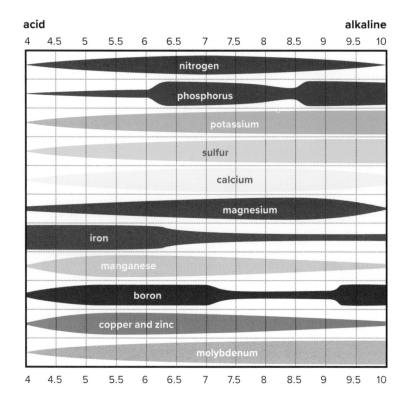

acid   alkaline

4   4.5   5   5.5   6   6.5   7   7.5   8   8.5   9   9.5   10

nitrogen

phosphorus

potassium

sulfur

calcium

magnesium

iron

manganese

boron

copper and zinc

molybdenum

4   4.5   5   5.5   6   6.5   7   7.5   8   8.5   9   9.5   10

Soil pH affects nutrient availability, with more nutrients available in the middle part of the range.

How to Adjust Soil pH

Soil pH is regional because it is determined by the mineral ingredients or native geology of the site, making it difficult to alter on a large scale. We can, however, adjust soil pH in discrete locations. The general rule of thumb is to add lime to raise the pH of acidic soil and add sulfur to lower the pH of alkaline soil.

Imagine that you are growing an alkaline lover like boxwood next to an acid lover like azalea. It shouldn't be surprising that one might do better than the other due to the pH of the soil. In that case, the best thing to do is adjust the pH around the root zone of the plant that is struggling. Soil pH can be increased, and hence the acidity decreased, around a boxwood shrub by amending the soil with limestone. It's as simple as tossing a cup or two of pelletized lime around the roots in the spring. This will sweeten the soil just enough to keep the boxwood happy.

Conversely, pH can be lowered, hence acidity increased, by applying pelletized sulfur to the soil. Sulfur is slow to assimilate into the soil, though, so the pH may take up to a year to change. In either case avoid powders, as they are messy and difficult to spread evenly.

While lime is good for lawns, which perform best in alkaline soils, the amount needed to effect a large-scale change is prohibitive. Over many years liming your lawn can make a difference, but mostly it makes the gardener feel better for trying.

Getting Your Soil Tested

Soil testing is simple, and sending a sample to a local lab will get you a lot of useful information and advice. University or county extension services in your area are often the best resource for soil tests, and their fees tend to be reasonable. Check websites and request a soil test submission form. While store-bought test kits can provide general indications as to the quality of a soil, they are not nearly as accurate or comprehensive as professional soil tests. When you send your soil to a lab, you can also request more advanced tests, such as screening for heavy metals or other contaminants.

Determine the type of gardening proposed for each area of your yard, such as vegetable garden, lawn, flower bed, or shrub bed. Collect samples to be tested from each area so the testing agency can make specific recommendations for the proposed use. Take samples from several spots in each specific gardening area by digging down six to ten inches to collect a cup of soil. Mix the samples for that area together and send the required amount indicated on the test instructions. Send the soil when it's fresh and follow all other instructions on the submission form. You should receive the results in two to three weeks.

What a soil test measures

Here is what a basic soil test measures:

Texture The exact proportion of sand, silt, and clay, and a specific class name such as clay loam, sandy loam, or loam. If the word *loam* is in the class name, the soil is workable.

CEC (cation exchange capacity) The maximum quantity of total nutrient cations the soil can hold and that are available for exchange. A CEC of 25 or more is considered quite fertile.

Nutrients In parts per million, the levels of phosphorus, potassium, sulfur, calcium, magnesium, sodium, boron, zinc, manganese, copper, and iron in the soil. Nitrogen is not measured because its levels fluctuate seasonally.

Sending a soil sample to a local lab will get you lots of useful information and advice.

Organic matter Percentage of decaying plant matter by volume, optimally 4 to 5 percent. Neglected soils, like that beneath a lawn, have less than 1 percent, and sometimes none at all, which means the soil is dead.

Soil pH A measure of the acidity or alkalinity of the soil on a scale from 0 to 14, with 7 as neutral. The lower the number, the more acid the soil.

To amend or not to amend?

What are you going to do with your soil test results? Once you get to know your soil, you will have a choice: grow plants that will thrive in the soil you have or create the soil preferred by the plants you want to grow.

When working with any limiting factor, be it pH, soil texture, field capacity, or fertility, it is often easier to grow plants that like the conditions already present. It's simpler to match the plant to the soil than it is to change the soil to suit the plant. Working with what nature provides is always more sustainable, but it takes time to reach that stage with your soil. Popular misconceptions and

What Can You Compost?

GREENS FOR NITROGEN

spent flowers

weeds from seeds (composting will kill the seeds)

lawn and garden clippings

veggie scraps

fruit peels and rinds

coffee grounds

loose tea

fish and fish skin

bird poop

livestock manures

seaweed

wine and beer

BROWNS FOR CARBON

dry leaves

twigs

bark

newsprint with black ink only

shredded cardboard

paper bags

paper towels and tissues

dryer lint

hair and pet fur

nail clippings

coffee filters, tea bags

pasta and rice,
  uncooked or with
  no sauce

stale bread and crackers

NOT ALLOWED

dairy products

meat and bones

eggs

nut butters

oil and grease

twist ties

rubber bands

glossy magazines

newsprint with colored inks

diseased plants

weeds from roots

cigarette butts

These common items in your weekly waste are neither green nor brown, but they are okay to add occasionally, a handful at a time:

eggshells (a source of calcium)

fish bones (a source of calcium)

fireplace ash (a source of potassium)

misguided maintenance practices often leave the soil so degraded that some amendments are necessary to start. Adding compost to promote a living soil and improve soil structure is the best first step. Over time it comes down to how much work you want to do and how much control over the garden you want to wield.

Making Compost

Knowing the importance of organic matter in our soil, we should find a way to add it to our gardens. Over time, a layer of humus will develop on any soil if the plant parts that fall to the ground are left in place. This happens in the fields and forests of the world. All too often, however, it does not happen in gardens. Gardeners are sometimes too tidy, more inclined to pick up a stray stick than leave it where it lies. We're often too organized and want things neat and clean. Nature, however, likes things messy—dirty, one might say—and dirt wants humus. Happily, gardeners can have their humus and keep clean too by making and spreading compost on the ground.

The basic recipe

There are multiple techniques to make compost, but they all basically amount to combining nitrogen-rich materials (greens) with carbon-rich ingredients (browns) and the microbes that break them down. In the presence of air and

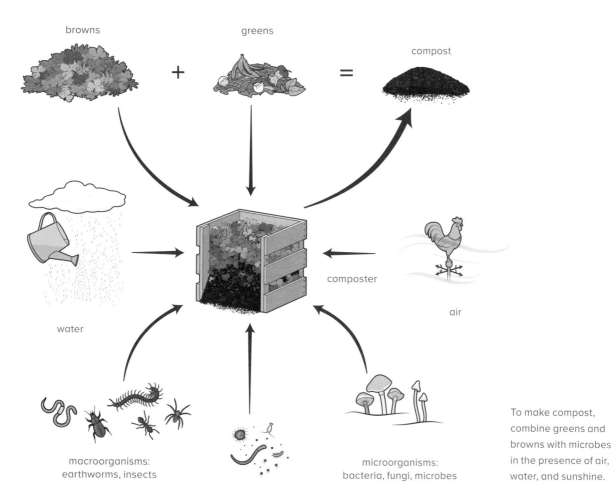

browns + greens = compost

water

composter

air

macroorganisms:
earthworms, insects

microorganisms:
bacteria, fungi, microbes

To make compost, combine greens and browns with microbes in the presence of air, water, and sunshine.

water to keep the microbes alive, and enough sunshine to keep them warm enough to thrive, compost, like humus, happens. The gardener simply supplies the ingredients. When it comes to the microbes, don't be fooled into buying "compost starter." You can find all you need in a small shovelful of decent soil.

Greens and browns come in all shapes and sizes, but the smaller the pieces, the more quickly they decompose. Dense ingredients like citrus peels and corncobs take a long time, so add them sparingly. Start with a 50-50 mixture of greens and browns by volume, being sure to balance out nitrogen-rich greens like lawn clippings and manures with high-carbon browns like cardboard and wood chips. Some ready-made green-and-brown combos are used teabags, coffee grounds with filter, and bird poop with the cage liner paper. If the pile gets smelly, add more browns. If nothing seems to be happening, add more greens and

a shovelful of soil to boost the microbes. Over time you will learn how to strike the right balance and keep the pile active.

There are restrictions on what should be added to a home garden compost pile. While anything organic—like feces, meat, and cheese—is technically compostable, the home composter should avoid these. Dairy products and oils can easily turn a small pile rancid, and while livestock manures are fine, certain feces are not. A simple rule to follow: if the poop comes from an herbivore it's safe, but poop from carnivores and omnivores isn't. So keep your cat and dog droppings out of the composter.

Once the pile is cooking, a steady supply of ready humus can be harvested every few weeks. The completed compost will settle down to the bottom of the pile or composter where it can be retrieved.

Containers for composting

You have a choice of containers for composting. Each type has its advantages and disadvantages.

Open bins provide adequate space for the volume of greens and browns produced in the average suburban garden. The three-sided bin can be built with sides made of wood slats, wire, hay bales, or cement blocks, three to five feet high and wide. Add browns and greens in equal measure and let them biodegrade together. Speed the process by turning the pile every few weeks with a pitchfork. This sifts the completed compost to the bottom of the pile, where it can be gathered for use. A three-bin system allows the avid gardener to tend multiple compost piles in progressive stages of decomposition. In time, bins made of wood or bales will rot and fall apart, so unless you use cement blocks be prepared to build the bin again in several years. ▼

Composters are great for small gardens and people who want to reduce their weekly waste by composting kitchen scraps. These self-contained units can be set on the ground outside near a back door or deck for easy year-round access. They come ventilated to allow air and water in but should be placed in a partially shaded spot, since full sun will overheat the microbes inside. Add greens and browns through the opening on top and harvest the completed compost through the convenient door located where it settles at the bottom. ▶

▲ **Heaps** are the lazy way to compost. Best for large gardens with plenty of room to work, they're based on the idea that everything organic biodegrades sooner or later. Find an out-of-the-way spot for your heap, behind a shed or in the woods. Here lawn and garden clippings, branches, twigs, and autumn leaves can be piled up year after year to turn into usable compost. No need to turn the heap, but you will need to dig down to the bottom to harvest the humus when the time comes.

▲ **Tumblers** are ideal for urban gardens. I recommend them to gardeners who are reluctant to set up a composter or bin on their rooftop or terrace. These self-contained units keep things clean and are sealed so critters, including vermin, won't get a whiff of the kitchen scraps inside. Tumblers work fast, creating a batch of compost in two or three weeks, but they work best when you have enough materials for a complete batch. One disadvantage of tumblers is that if you add compostables daily, the completed compost is difficult to harvest since different materials in the tumbler are at different stages of decomposition. Two-chamber tumblers solve this issue.

Pits are similar to bins but simpler because you don't have to build walls, you just dig holes. Pits are less obtrusive, since the composting takes place mostly at or below ground level, and highly adaptable, as you can dig bigger pits or fill in old ones as your needs change. The best benefit with pits is that the newly added compostables are in more immediate contact with the microbes in the soil, providing effective results with minimal effort.

My Pit Composting Method, Step by Step

If you have the room for it, try the three-pit method I use to produce compost. It takes about a year for the material in each successive pit to decompose.

Step 1, spring: Dig a pit

For kitchen scraps from a family of four with a modest-size garden, make the pit four feet square and two feet deep. Pile the soil to one side of the pit, making sure there is space for two additional pits adjacent to the first.

Step 2, spring into summer: Layer compostables

Start with greens covered with enough browns to equal their volume. Next, cover both with soil from the pile, making sure no greens can be seen. It's okay if some browns show. Continue to layer greens, browns, soil, greens, browns, soil. There's no need to make complete layers each time. When adding just a few greens, add a little bit of browns and cover with just enough soil.

Step 3, summer into fall: Dig the second pit

The first pit is full when the pile rises a foot or more above ground level. That's when it's time to dig another pit. Pile the new soil with what's left from digging the first pit and use it as you continue to layer greens, browns, and soil. Keep adding material until the end of the season.

Step 4, autumn through winter: Dig the third pit

Add the excavated soil to the previous pile. Keep filling the second pit until it too is a foot above ground level, then start layering greens, browns, and soil in the third pit. This will carry you through the winter. Decomposition will slow or stall during winter months that are consistently cold, at or below 40 degrees F, but since there will be no garden clippings, just kitchen scraps, you shouldn't run out of room.

Step 5, spring into summer: Harvest the first pit

You will notice that the first pit has settled. This is because the materials in it have decomposed into humus. This is finished compost. Dig it out and use it in the garden by top-dressing an inch thick around the roots of your favorite plants, or add it where the soil needs replenishing, such as a vegetable patch. Use this empty pit to start layering fresh greens, browns, and soil once the third pit is full. When the first pit is full again, the compost in the second pit will be ready for harvest. Continue the rotation, layering, waiting, and harvesting pit after pit, using the compost as it becomes available or storing it in an open bin for later use.

Options for apartment dwellers

Gardeners who live in apartments or high-rise buildings and grow plants in pots on a terrace might lament their inability to compost effectively at home, but there are ways to do it.

◀ **Vermicomposting** is composting with worms, and it can be done in a plastic bin in your closet. It employs specialized worms, so don't go outside and dig some out of the ground and think that will work. It's not a method recommended for the squeamish, but for those determined to compost indoors it's a handy option.

▲ **Community composting** is offered by many cities and towns. Collected separately during weekly trash pickup, everyone's compostables go to a large facility where they are placed in long piles called windrows. The materials biodegrade, and the completed compost is available free or for a nominal fee.

Buying compost

When I was an estate gardener in charge of improving the soil of an eighteen-acre garden, we fell short of having the greens and browns to make enough compost to replenish the beds each season. The same is true for most new gardens. The yearly kitchen scraps and newsprint from an average family won't add up to more than a bushel or two of completed compost. Even adding garden clippings and autumn leaves won't produce enough to prepare a new landscape or edibles bed. That's when we shop for compost.

Sold by the bag or in bulk, store-bought compost comes in many flavors, made from manures, seaweed, bark, even lobster shells and spent mushroom substrate made of straw or sawdust. The initial ingredients correlate directly to the quality and characteristics of the completed product, making certain composts preferred for specific crops. But mostly it's a matter of personal preference. Some gardeners use only manures, while others swear by mushroom blends.

To figure out how much compost you'll need to cover an area an inch deep, multiply the length and width of the area in feet by .08 (a twelfth of a foot, or one inch). The result will be the quantity in cubic feet. For example, eight cubic feet is enough to amend one hundred square feet of garden.

Compost is regional, so look to local suppliers. Bulk deliveries cost less per cubic foot compared to bags, but bags are easier to handle. The best time to top-dress existing beds is early spring, before the plants have emerged. New beds should be amended before planting with enough to cover the bed with one inch of compost.

Soilless Mixes for Container Gardening

Maintaining healthy soil is the first step toward success in the garden. On the ground we replenish depleted organic matter by top-dressing with compost we either make or buy. Gardening in containers poses a different challenge, most notably the fact that when we grow plants in pots we don't grow in soil, we grow in potting mixes. In fact, most potting mixes contain no soil at all. They are devised using combinations of ingredients that provide the three key attributes of a healthy soil: proper drainage (structure), moisture retention (field capacity), and ample fertility (cation exchange).

The right potting medium is the mix that matches the plants you intend to grow. Store-bought mixes typically fall short of perfection but can easily be improved. The main problem with bagged mixes is inadequate drainage. Start with a basic bag of potting mix or potting soil. Add

bagged perlite (an igneous rock heated until it expands into tiny, lightweight balls that look like Styrofoam) to improve drainage. Add compost or an organic fertilizer to increase fertility. Specialty mixes for cacti or tropical plants are available, but amend them as well, adding perlite for drainage and compost for fertility.

I took soil for granted at the beginning of my gardening education. I'm embarrassed to say I almost failed my university soil science class, but like many struggles in the garden, near failure led to a greater appreciation of the subject matter. I soon discovered that the beauty of what takes place among the roots is equal to the attractions displayed by the shoots.

Knowing how soil works is such a fundamental part of gardening, it's difficult to overemphasize the importance of the information presented in this chapter. What you have learned can be extended to all forms of gardening, from establishing landscape plants around the house to growing edibles, raising cut flowers, or tending a patch of native forest. If balancing the roots and the shoots is our goal, understanding the environment where plant roots grow increases the intuitive command new gardeners develop with each successive season.

With soil tested and understood, the time for planting arrives—and the excitement of selecting from the myriad of available plants those that we ultimately choose to grow.

◄ When you grow plants in containers, the challenge becomes picking the right potting mix.

plant
selection

Matching Plants to Place

You can't be a gardener without an intimate knowledge of plants.

Plant selection is as important as proper planting skills, and together they are vital if you are to have any hope of horticultural success. You should know why you want to grow a plant and have a place to grow it. You should take the time to learn each plant's preferences before you buy it. How cold can it get? How much sun does it want? In what soil does it grow best? Good gardening relies upon your focused engagement with plants. This ultimately shapes your experiences in the garden, and everyone will agree that gardening is more fun when your plants thrive.

"Right Plant, Right Place"

"Right plant, right place" is a common cliché in gardening publications, but like most clichés, it encapsulates a simple truth. Choose a plant that's right for the purpose at hand and plant it in a location best suited to its survival so that purpose can be fulfilled. Our desire to possess a particular plant often leads to poor plant selection, wasted effort, and ultimately heartache. Use your head instead and base your plant selections on four criteria: purpose, hardiness, exposure, and soil.

Purpose

Determine the purpose of your plants by asking why you want to grow them. What will they do for you? Do you want flowers for beauty, or are you growing food, such as vegetables, herbs, and fruits? Determine the purpose of each plant by asking to what extent it will contribute to two main categories of gardening: ornamental landscaping and growing edibles (realizing that some edibles, like kale, chives, and blueberries, can be grown for their ornamental features).

After the ornamental or edible question is answered, consider form. Plants come in many shapes, and the shape should support the purpose of the plant. For example, if the goal is to create a place to sit in the shade, consider a spreading and not a columnar tree. Canopy trees, like beech or oak, have branches that create a ceiling, while screening trees, like spruce or pine, have branches that create a wall. If the goal is to grow green beans, decide between bush or pole beans based on the usable space in your plot.

Select a size by determining what fits best. For example, a sugar maple is too big for a small plot, while a Japanese maple could be just right. It's a common mistake for beginning gardeners to underestimate the space a large plant will require. Research and learn a plant's mature size before deciding where it goes.

To find out a plant's requirements and characteristics, you can search online using the plant's botanical name, look up the plant in a plant encyclopedia, consult cooperative extension publications, or ask other gardeners and plant professionals who have grown the plant in your region.

Hardiness

Hardiness refers to a plant's ability to survive the winter. The US Department of Agriculture has divided the United States and southern Canada into eleven different hardiness zones in its map available online. On hardiness zone maps, the higher the hardiness zone number, the warmer the average low temperature in winter in that zone. Sometimes, however, temperatures drop below normal. Most winters they don't, but they could, and if they do, plants that are less hardy suffer. When selecting plants other than annuals, always choose those at your hardiness zone number or lower. For example, if you live in zone 5b in the United States, don't plant anything with a hardiness zone number of 6a or higher.

Hardiness zone maps are available for much of the world. To find yours, start at plantmaps.com.

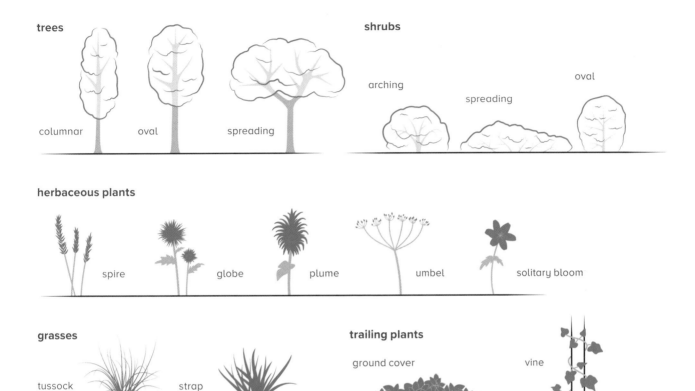

trees

columnar

oval

spreading

shrubs

arching

spreading

oval

herbaceous plants

spire

globe

plume

umbel

solitary bloom

grasses

tussock

strap

trailing plants

ground cover

vine

The form of a plant should be chosen to support its purpose in the garden—spreading trees for shade, columnar trees for windbreaks and screens, for example.

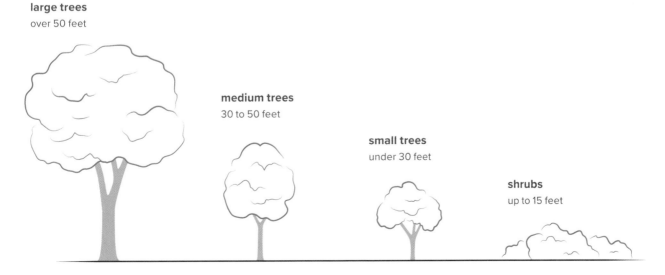

large trees
over 50 feet

medium trees
30 to 50 feet

small trees
under 30 feet

shrubs
up to 15 feet

Choose a plant that when mature will fit the space you have.

Gardener's Glossary

Hardiness is a plant's ability to survive winter temperatures.

A **hardiness zone** is a climatic zone based on the average annual low temperature.

Microclimates are places in a garden where temperatures are warmer or colder than normal and where plants from outside the garden's zone can sometimes be grown.

Zone busting is successfully growing a plant outside its hardiness zone.

Cultural requirements are a plant's water, soil, and sun needs.

Exposure is the amount of sun a plant prefers.

Deciduous trees and shrubs lose their leaves in winter, while **evergreens** hang on to them.

Broadleaf evergreens are evergreen trees and shrubs like holly and camellia with leaves that have a flat, relatively broad surface.

Coniferous evergreens are evergreen trees and shrubs like pines, firs, cedars, and junipers that have needlelike or scalelike leaves.

Bedding plants are annuals, usually flowering, grown in masses as a ground cover.

Gardens also have microclimates, places where the typical temperature is either warmer or colder than normal and where conditions vary enough to affect the survival of a plant. Warmer microclimates are found near the radiant heat of buildings and on south-facing sunny slopes. Even a laundry dryer venting out of a house can create a microclimate where less-than-hardy plants will survive the winter. Colder microclimates occur in low spots where the air sinks or in a northern exposure such as in the

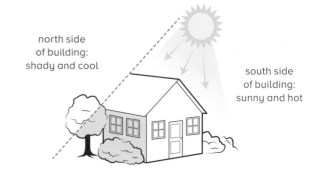

north side of building: shady and cool

south side of building: sunny and hot

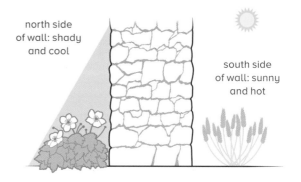

north side of wall: shady and cool

south side of wall: sunny and hot

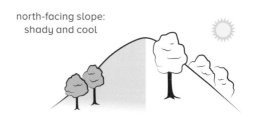

north-facing slope: shady and cool

south-facing slope: sunny and hot

hilltop: frigid winds

cold pocket: cold air collects

Microclimates can affect the survival of plants in your garden and let you get away with growing a plant outside its hardiness zone.

shadow of a tall building. Knowledge of microclimates empowers gardeners to do something called zone busting, successfully growing a plant outside its hardiness zone.

Exposure

Exposure refers to the amount of sun a plant prefers. Matching a plant's sun preference to the actual sun available is crucial if you want it to thrive. Different gardens, indeed different parts of a garden, are exposed to different amounts of sun, and while many plants can tolerate a range of sun, all plants have levels of light they perform best in.

Sun energy is the driving force for all plant growth. Many sun-loving plants can tolerate shade and vice versa, but a plant will live up to its full potential only when grown in the conditions it is best suited to. Consider boxwood or viburnum. A boxwood can survive in the shade, but it won't thrive. It will grow thin because less than full sun doesn't drive enough photosynthesis to make the sugars needed to fuel growth for a lush plant. A viburnum will also survive in sun or shade, but in shade it grows spindly. With fewer leaves it can't gather enough sun energy to make flowers, and though the plant doesn't die, it also doesn't bloom.

In general, canopy trees want full sun while understory trees and shrubs tolerate shade. Many shrubs, however, also want full sun, so it is important to consider the future growth of these plants and how the future canopy will affect sun exposure. What was once in full sun can turn shady after several years. I tell my garden design students, "Plants are not furniture." You can't put them in place and say you're done. All plants grow and change over time, and so does your garden. Keep that in mind.

In an edibles garden, a dearth of sun is disastrous. Most food plants need a lot of energy to grow strong enough to flower and fruit. You may get your melon or eggplant to grow leaves in part sun, but will it bear fruit? Maybe, but not like it would in all-day sun. If you must grow edibles in limited sun, grow those that don't fruit from flowers and need less energy to make the parts you eat—leaf and root vegetables like lettuce, mint, carrots, and beets.

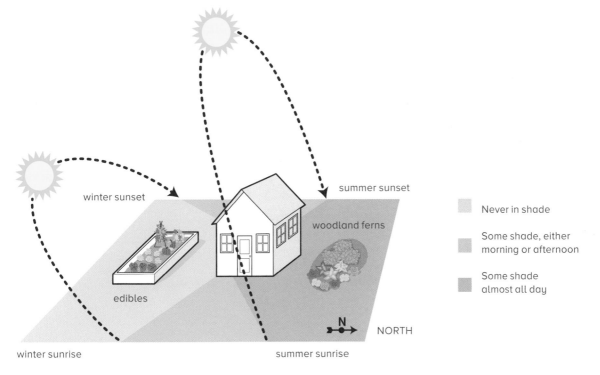

Different parts of a property offer different amounts of sun, and plants will do best where their exposure needs are met.

To determine whether a plant will like sun or shade, look at the leaves. Plants with big leaves, like hosta and Japanese aralia, typically prefer shady spots. Extensive surface area means plenty of chloroplasts to power growth with limited sunlight. Plants with minimal leaf area, such as conifers like pines, do well in sun. With limited surface area, they want a full day of sunshine to gather enough energy for good growth. Many sun lovers, like lavender and privet, have oils or waxes on the surface of their leaves that work a little like sun block and also limit transpiration. Plants with thin or delicate foliage, like ferns, can be assumed to thrive in shady spots where sunlight is dappled, indirect, or diffuse.

Levels of sun exposure specified on plant tags and in online and print sources are based on how many hours of direct sunlight a plant needs to receive each day during the growing season. The time of day the sun strikes also makes a difference. Morning sun (eastern exposure) is gentle, allowing the plant to wake up gradually. Late-day sun (western exposure) is hot and harsh. It can sap a plant's strength if the plant isn't an absolute sun lover like aster or sage. Midday sun is the strongest and will power photosynthesis most efficiently.

In addition, shade can be dappled or deep. Deep shade is no direct sun at all, like in the shadow of a tall building or beneath the dense canopy of evergreen trees. Dappled shade means there is sunlight, but it's filtered through the leaves of a tree or the slats of a structure. Stand beneath an open-canopy tree like a honey locust to experience dappled shade.

 full sun = six or more hours of direct sunlight per day

 part sun / part shade = three to six hours of direct sunlight per day

 shade = three or fewer hours of direct sunlight per day

Shade can be either deep (left) or dappled (right).

Leaves tell you a lot about a plant's sun preference.

How to Map Your Yard's Sun Exposure

Determining the sun exposure of your yard is tricky because the amount of sunlight reaching the ground changes over the course of a day and throughout the year. Unless you live on the equator, the position of the sun in the sky changes from season to season. It's higher in the summer and lower in the winter. This means a section of your garden that's in shade in April could be in full sun come July, and then in shade again in October. Deciduous trees drop their leaves, so it may be sunny beneath a chestnut tree in March but in deep shade by May after the leaves emerge.

Making a sun map of your garden is especially useful if you are new to the property or are planning extensive changes to the garden. Do it on a sunny day around the time of the summer solstice (the longest day of the year, which occurs around June 21 in the Northern Hemisphere), and once in the early spring or late fall when the deciduous trees have no leaves.

Here's how:

1. On graph paper, sketch a map of your property, including a footprint of the house, outbuildings, and every garden bed, hedge, and tree.

2. Go out a few times during the day and draw the shade outlines on your map. Aim to go out early morning, midmorning, noon, midafternoon, and late afternoon.

Alternatively, you could use an online tool like **FindMyShadow.com.**

A sun map of your garden tracks the changes in sun exposure throughout the day. ▶

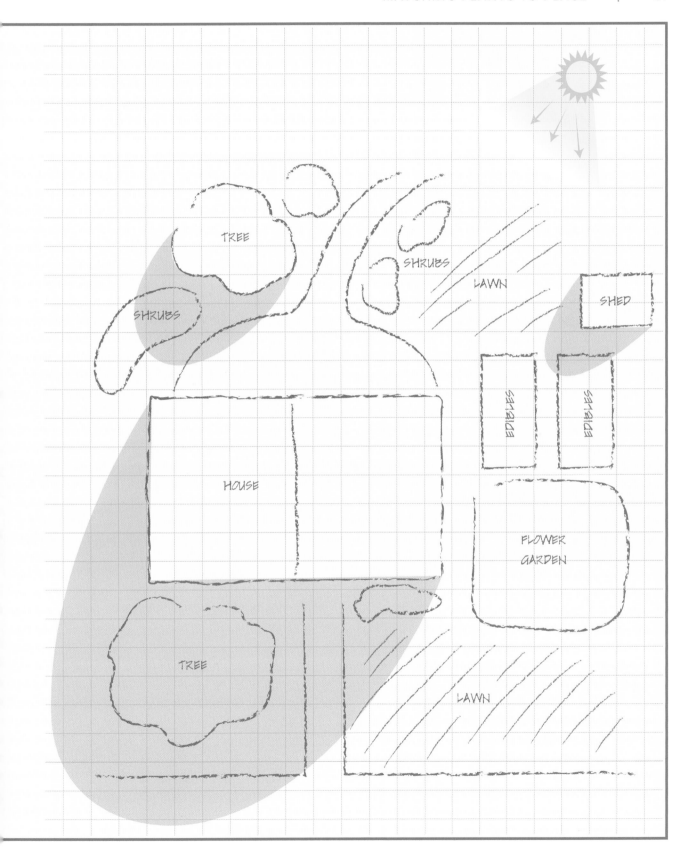

Soil

Soil type is different all over the world but plants grow everywhere, so no matter what kind of soil your garden has, unless it is toxic or otherwise polluted, there are plants suited to it. As discussed in the previous chapter, soil can be improved, but you still must work with the type of soil you have.

As a key cultural requirement for all plants, soil (with its particular texture, fertility, field capacity, and pH) sets limits on the types of plants you can grow. In sandy soil, for example, plants like succulents or sage that prefer sharp drainage and lower fertility will work. Soils with high clay content are very fertile, making them great for nutrient-hungry plants like peonies or sweet corn. Most evergreens—broadleaf plants like rhododendrons and hollies, and all conifers, such as pine and spruce—are acid lovers. They prefer low pH soils, from 5.5 to 6.5. On the opposite end of the spectrum, lawns and boxwoods do better in less acidic, more alkaline soils, with a pH of 6.5 and higher. Plants grown for fruit and flowers will perform best in soil with a pH higher than 6, when phosphorus becomes readily available for exchange.

The pH Preferences of Popular Plants

EDIBLES

4.0–5.0 blueberries

4.8–6.5 potatoes

5.0–6.0 strawberries

5.0–8.0 kale

5.5–6.5 apples, beans, carrots

5.8–7.0 beets

6.0–6.5 celery, peppers

6.0–7.0 asparagus, broccoli, cabbage, corn, eggplant, lettuce, onions, tomatoes

6.0–8.0 cucumbers, currants, peas, radishes, squash

TREES, SHRUBS, AND VINES

4.0–5.5 camellia

5.0–6.0 azalea, birch, chestnut, clethra, fir, heather, hemlock, holly, magnolia, pine, rhododendron

5.5–6.5 gardenia, larch

5.5–7.0 white oak, yew

6.0–7.0 beech, juniper, red oak, witch hazel

6.0–8.0 acacia, arborvitae, ash, butterfly bush, cherry, cotoneaster, deutzia, dogwood, elm, English ivy, eucalyptus, forsythia, hibiscus, hydrangea, lilac, linden, maple, poplar, privet, spirea, viburnum, willow, wisteria

HERBACEOUS FLOWERS AND FERNS

5.0–6.0 gayfeather

5.0–7.0 wood fern

5.0–8.0 pachysandra

5.5–6.5 coreopsis, lupine

6.0–7.0 ageratum, bee balm, sage

6.0–8.0 alyssum, anemone, aster, astilbe, bellflower, buttercup, Christmas fern, chrysanthemum, clematis, columbine, coneflower, dahlia, daylily, dianthus, forget-me-not, foxglove, gaillardia, garden phlox, geranium, gypsophila, heliotrope, iris, lungwort, maidenhair fern, nasturtium, pansy, poppy, primrose, Solomon's seal, stonecrop, sunflower, sweet pea, verbena, violet, zinnia

The internet is a great resource for finding appropriate plants for the conditions offered by your garden. Search using a phrase like "hardy evergreen shrubs for moist shade" or "drought-tolerant perennials for full sun."

The purpose of an ornamental garden is to create beauty around your home.

Planning an Ornamental Garden

If your objective is creating beauty around your home, your challenge is to select plants that work within the parameters of your hardiness zone, sun exposure, and soil type and come together in a harmonious whole. These elements are typically found in an ornamental garden:

Canopy—the mature trees that form the ceiling of an outdoor room.

Understory—the shrub layer or plants of medium height that help define spaces.

Ground cover—the layer of plants, usually herbaceous but sometimes woody, that blankets the ground.

Herbaceous border—a garden bed that includes a combination of herbaceous annuals, biennials, and perennials.

Mixed border—a garden bed that includes a combination of trees, shrubs, and ground covers.

Foundation planting—a group of trees, shrubs, and/or ground covers used to blend a building with the surrounding landscape or obscure ugly features of the architecture.

Hardscape—structural elements like sidewalks, patios, and arbors that complement the plantings.

When it comes to plant combinations, copy what works. Browse through magazines and books or visit great gardens for inspiration and ideas. Then combine the same plants in your own garden. And remember a few simple design rules:

- Plants of one color massed together have more impact than single plants of different colors.

- Plants repeated throughout the garden provide a sense of rhythm and unity, while a plant that contrasts in form, color, and/or texture can provide interest and accentuate the rest.

- Single specimen plants serve as focal points to direct our attention, guiding our eyes and in turn our feet as we move through a garden.

Remember that gardens, unlike other works of art, are never finished. They literally grow and change with each passing year, month, week, day—even hour. Stay open to new ideas and be fearless. My approach when it comes to home gardeners and design is that we are all entitled to our own taste. If you love it, go for it!

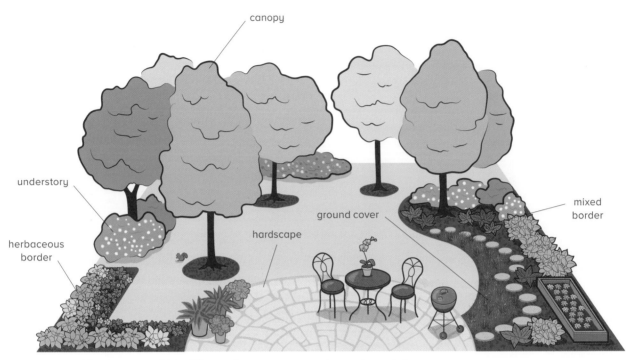

canopy

understory

herbaceous
border

hardscape

ground cover

mixed
border

An ornamental landscape combines different elements to create a harmonious whole.

A Note about Natives

Plants that are indigenous to your region are called natives. They represent a growing collection of cultivated plants available to gardeners seeking to promote sustainability and biodiversity in the home landscape. Native plants are automatically suited to regional environmental conditions, making them valuable alternatives to popular nonnative garden species that require more work to successfully grow. Natives also provide habitat for local wildlife, including pollinators like butterflies and bees, as well as other beneficial insects and animals that join with the plants to promote a healthy, balanced ecosystem.

Copy appealing plant combinations you see in magazines, books, or great gardens.

Trees and shrubs

Trees are the feature players in a garden. They set the stage for future growing conditions, like sun or shade, and lend an air of maturity to any landscape as they age, creating the ceiling above an outdoor space. Large trees like maple, cedar, and oak serve as signature pieces and therefore should be planted first because large trees take many years to mature into significant specimens. Consider all four seasons when selecting trees. Think about spring flowers, summer form, fall foliage, and winter interest from bark or evergreen needles. The rule is to choose your trees carefully but plant them right away.

Shrubs are the supporting cast, though sometimes they can steal the show, especially in small gardens where space for large trees is limited. Deciduous or evergreen, shrubs bring a unique blend of foliage and flower to any planting. Leaf shape can range from tight needles to giant blades, in colors from every green imaginable to blue, red, purple, and silver. Flowers span the spectrum of hues and unique shapes and sizes. Planted in masses or individually, shrubs add depth and interest to any planting bed while forming the backbone of the garden.

Ten Favorite Small Trees for Gardens

DECIDUOUS
crabapple
crape myrtle
dogwood
Eastern redbud
Japanese maple
ornamental cherry
star magnolia

EVERGREEN
Hinoki cypress
mountain mahogany
mountain pine

Ten Trees for Multiseason Interest

DECIDUOUS
Amur cherry
Chinese tree lilac
Japanese stewartia
mountain ash
paperbark maple
river birch
snakebark maple
white birch

EVERGREEN
Korean fir
Colorado blue spruce

Evergreen Trees and Shrubs for Hedging and Screening

arborvitae
Canadian hemlock
English laurel
green spire euonymous
holly
Japanese cedar
juniper
leatherleaf viburnum
mountain laurel
photinia
privet

Ten Favorite Flowering Shrubs

DECIDUOUS
elderberry
fothergilla
Japanese spirea
mock orange
smokebush
viburnum

EVERGREEN
azalea
camellia
ceanothus
mountain laurel
oleander

Trees and shrubs form the backbone of a garden. ▲

Herbaceous perennials cover the ground with a diversity
of foliage and flowers. ▶

Roses, though beloved for their blooms, are not great garden plants. While they look beautiful in full flower, they tend to turn into ugly sticks with ratty leaves later in the season, even in perfect growing conditions with expert care. I recommend growing hybrid tea roses in an out-of-the-way spot where they can look great in early summer but be unremarked the rest of the year. Varieties like shrub or rugosa roses tend to look better longer.

Herbaceous perennials

Both supporting cast and scenery extras, herbaceous perennials flesh out ornamental plantings by covering the ground with a diversity of foliage and flowers. There was a time when gardeners grew just a few kinds of herbaceous perennials, such as peonies, lilies, sweet peas, and poppies, but today hundreds of new herbaceous perennials have become available to home gardeners, with new varieties released every year. However, like every gardener I have a short list of favorites based on reliable performance and ease of care.

Ten Favorite Perennials for Dry Sun

catmint
coneflower
coreopsis
daylilies
penstemon
rudbeckia
salvia
sedum
switchgrass
yarrow

Ten Favorite Perennials for Moist Shade

arisaema
fatsia
ferns
hosta
Japanese forest grass
mayapple
sedge
Solomon's seal
toadlily
wild ginger

Ten Perennials to Grow for Foliage

barrenwort
brunnera
coral bells
hosta
lady's mantle
lamium
ligularia
lungwort
ornamental grasses
rodgersia

If you live in an area with cold winters, you can grow tender perennials, such as dahlias, cannas, ornamental gingers, and others, as long as you dig the large fleshy roots out of the ground in the autumn and store them in an unheated garage or cellar, then plant them in the garden again come spring. I pack mine in cardboard boxes filled with dry potting mix between layers of burlap.

Annuals used as bedding plants offer nonstop color all summer.

Annuals

Gardeners use annuals for season-long color. Unlike perennials, annual plants keep blooming from spring until frost, so they have a lot to offer. Many tropical species—crotons, for example—provide unique and colorful foliage. Best of all, annuals allow you to try something different each year, keeping your garden fresh and lively. Some annuals, like petunias, need to have old flowers removed in order to rebloom, but others, like impatiens, repeat bloom without pruning, making them valuable easy-care additions for borders and pots.

Annuals can be used in two ways: as bedding plants or dropped in among trees, shrubs, and herbaceous perennials. Bedding annuals suggest a formal garden: a carpet of pink and white wax begonias beneath an old magnolia tree, for example. Annuals dropped in among perennials add depth and interest to the garden. Their nonstop flowers and perpetually lush foliage draw attention away from tired shrubs or slow-to-emerge plants and late bloomers.

Ten Easy-to-Grow Annuals

begonia
browallia
coleus
fuchsia
impatiens
marigold
million bells
torenia
verbena
zinnia

Bulbs

Bulbs add an extra layer of interest and sophistication to any landscape. Spring bloomers, like daffodils, tulips, hyacinth, and crocus, are the easiest to include. Plant them in

Bulbs add an extra layer of seasonal interest.

areas where they will put on a show, then fade away as other plants emerge. Summer bloomers like lilies and ornamental onions work best as companion plants with other ground covers so their yellowing leaves are hidden once they finish flowering. Fall-flowering bulbs are uncommon, but hardy cyclamen is a fun one. The trick is to remember where you planted them so that you don't accidentally dig them up in the summertime when they are dormant.

Vines and climbers

Vines are especially useful for small gardens or where space is limited. Climbers grow up instead of out, and they look great scrambling across a wall or fence. Some vines fruit, most flower, but the best offer attractive, long-lasting foliage. Annual vines like morning glory provide quick and easy color, while perennial vines like clematis and ivy expand their coverage year by year. Perennial vines can be either evergreen, like star jasmine, or deciduous, like trumpet vine and wisteria.

Vines and climbers like this Japanese hydrangea vine soften walls and fences.

Every vine has a unique way of climbing, such as by twining, tendrils, or clinging roots. Be sure to match how a vine grows to what you want it to grow on. For example, clematis is a twiner, so it will go up a tree trunk or pole, but it won't scale a wall like Boston ivy will. An interesting way to use vines is to train them to climb down or scramble across the ground. Ivy makes a vigorous ground covering, and I have used climbing hydrangea as an attractive erosion control for steep slopes.

Favorite Vines and Climbers

DECIDUOUS

bougainvillea
clematis (most varieties)
climbing hydrangea (most varieties)
honeysuckle
hops
ivy (some varieties)
Japanese hydrangea vine
kiwi vine
rambling rose
sweet pea
trumpet vine
wisteria

EVERGREEN

clematis (some varieties)
climbing hydrangea (some varieties)
ivy (some varieties)
passion flower

Lawns

Traditional turfgrass lawns are unsustainable and ecologically irresponsible, requiring extensive irrigation, fertilizers, herbicides, and pesticides, and the ongoing use of noisy and air-polluting gasoline-powered equipment. In my opinion, turf lawns should be cultivated only as playing fields for sports. End of sermon. The fact is that people like and want lawns, so if you must have a lawn outside your house, be smart about it.

The best lawn is one well suited to your climate.

The best turfgrass is one that is well suited to your climate: warm season turf (zoysia and Bermuda) for warm climates; cool season turf (rye and fescue) for cooler climates; water lovers (St. Augustine) for regions with humid summers; drought-tolerant species (buffalo grass) for regions with dry summers. There is no appropriate turfgrass for desert climates.

It's easier to find the appropriate species of turfgrass for your climate as seed than as sod. Sod is for instant gratification, but a seeded lawn is much cheaper and easier to install. Be earth friendly and keep your lawn area to a bare minimum—no more than you can easily mow with a push reel mower.

A truly organic lawn is possible if you subscribe to the dictate "Anything green is good," including weeds. There are many lawn alternatives that require no mowing, irrigation, or chemicals to thrive, but they come with limitations as compared to traditional turfgrass. For example, lilyturf and creeping thyme won't stand up to foot traffic, while mints and clovers will, but they can become invasive.

Make your edible garden as simple or as elaborate as you need it to be.

Planning an Edible Garden

Edibles are plants grown for food, including vegetables, fruits, nuts, and herbs. Form follows function for most edible gardens, meaning the gardener chooses production over appearance. However, some kitchen gardens, called potagers, are laid out with fancy designs that include paths, wooden structures, and decorative plants. Dwarf fruit trees or flowering shrubs used as highlights or hedge enclosures can add an ornamental aspect to an edible garden. The use of ornamental edibles, like elephant kale or artichoke, is another fun way to add beauty to your food plot.

Vegetables

For vegetables, a ten-by-ten-foot plot is enough to kick things off. Start small, planting just one or two of each vegetable you fancy. Peppers, tomatoes, and summer squash are good bets for beginning gardeners. You'll be astonished at how many tomatoes you get from a single plant and how far a squash vine can spread. Plant greens like lettuce and kale and root vegetables like carrots and radishes in rows or squares of a dozen plants or more. These are cool-season plants, started in the spring and harvested before summer, making room for warm-season plants like eggplants and corn.

Ten Reliable Cool-Season Vegetables

broccoli

cabbage

carrots

cauliflower

kale

kohlrabi

onions

radishes

spinach

Swiss chard

Ten Popular Warm-Season Vegetables

bell peppers

cantaloupe

cucumbers

eggplant

green beans

summer squash

sweet corn

sweet potatoes

tomatoes

watermelon

Herbs

Grow herbs in pots or a raised bed close to your kitchen door. Most need excellent drainage and specific soils, which are easier to provide as potting mix in a container. Grown in a small enough pot, the entire plant can come into the kitchen for casual clipping, to extend the harvest into the winter, or as an aromatic addition to your décor. Annual herbs like sage and cilantro and perennial herbs like chives and thyme both have a place in a kitchen garden. I keep my annual herbs alive as long as possible, but sooner or later they must be harvested and either used right away or dried and stored in airtight canisters.

Ten Easy Herbs

basil

chives

cilantro

lemongrass

mint

parsley

rosemary

sage

tarragon

thyme

Fruiting woodies

Fruiting woody plants include fruit trees and vines, nut trees, and berries. Fruit and nut trees typically need full sun and well-draining soil, and come in a range of sizes. Dwarf varieties stay under ten feet tall and do well in containers. Semidwarf varieties reach fifteen feet tall, and standard varieties grow up to forty feet tall. Choose varieties that fit your space, are suited to your climate, and are bred for pest and disease resistance. Apples and peaches typically have more pest and disease problems than other fruits, while persimmons and figs are relatively care free. As part of a master plan, fruit and nut trees are valuable additions to any ornamental landscape.

Vines such as grapes and kiwis can also be ornamental but have a messiness factor to consider, so choose wisely where you use them. The romance of dining beneath a pergola draped in grape vines is quickly dispelled when a few ripe fruits drop on your head. Grow them on a dedicated structure instead, where you can harvest them easily and attend to their frequent pruning needs.

Berries are easy to grow but sometimes difficult to establish, taking several years before they fruit well. Blueberries are notoriously slow starters. Bramble berries, like raspberries and blackberries, take up a lot of space and spread by runners unless contained, while bushes like goji berry are easy to keep in bounds. Strawberries spread across the ground, so good drainage is key to keep them from rotting when it rains too much. Berry plants are often stripped clean of fruits by birds and chipmunks before the gardener gets a taste. Prevent this by growing them in a berry cage house or placing netting over the plants before the fruit ripens.

◀ Grow herbs by your kitchen door to make it easy to use them when cooking

Netting can help protect berry plants as their fruit ripens. ▼

How to Make a Planting Plan

Planting plans are useful because they help you envision your dream garden and develop a strategy to achieve it. A frequent lament from my garden design clients is how much money and time they wasted by installing their garden piecemeal. Save time and money by developing a plan that considers the garden as a whole.

Draw your plan to scale, one inch = ten feet for a full property master plan. (Properties five acres or larger require a larger scale: one inch = twenty feet or more.) Draw the plan on graph paper big enough so the entire garden fits and use a pencil so you can erase and correct mistakes. Take measurements directly outside with a measuring wheel or tape. Sketch the position of planting beds, trees, and shrubs in relation to structures and the property line.

Use a scale of one inch = five feet for smaller areas or when zooming in on plantings to indicate the precise location of smaller plants. This way you can determine the exact number of plants you will need to fill a space based on the species you choose and their projected mature sizes.

This basic planting plan for a sunny sitting garden with a stepping-stone path specifies the type and arrangement of plants to be used.

—————————————————

scale: 1 square = 1 foot

A. *Cornus sericea* 'Ivory Halo'
B. *Stachys byzantina* 'Silver Carpet'
C. *Geranium macorrhizum* 'Bevan's Variety'
D. *Liatris spicata* 'Kobold'
E. *Pelargonium* cultivars in pots
F. *Juniperus squamata* 'Blustar'
G. *Gaura lindheimeri* 'Siskiyou Pink'
H. *Buxus sempervirens* 'Jensen'
I. *Geum coccineum*
J. *Leucanthemum* ×*superbum* 'Becky'
K. *Clematis terniflora*
L. *Echinacea purpurea*

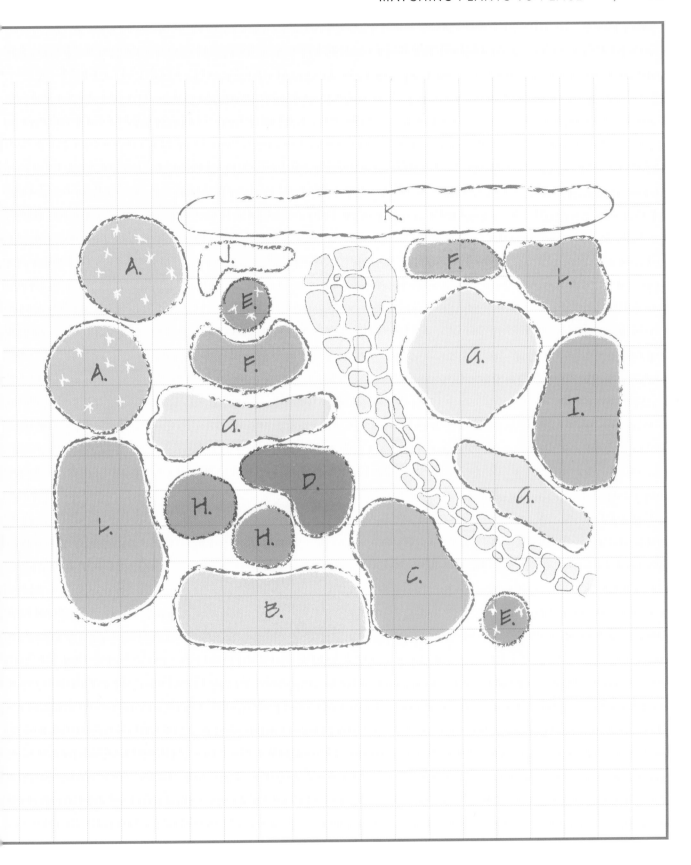

When and Where to Get Plants

Once you have a good idea of the plants you want to grow, it's time to start thinking about where you'll get them. The best season to buy plants is spring, and the best plant sources depend on the plants you're looking for.

Big box stores carry a good variety of popular plants at reasonable prices. If you know what you're looking for they can serve as a cost-saving resource, but buyer beware. Inadequate care of these plants while on the shelves is always a concern. Smart shoppers buy only plants delivered to the store that same day. This decreases the chance that the plants have been neglected.

Garden centers are the most popular source for plants. These stores buy plants wholesale from multiple growers and sell them retail to the public. Though more expensive than big box stores, garden centers have a better selection and a plant-savvy staff with whom you can develop friendly relations.

Nurseries, unlike garden centers, propagate the plants they sell. Run by professional horticulturists and silviculturists, nurseries often specialize, providing hard-to-find species to a discerning clientele while also supplying popular plants to retail garden centers.

Mail order is a great way to buy plants your local garden center doesn't carry. Circumspect gardeners limit themselves to mail-order nurseries within a two-or-three-hundred-mile radius from their garden. This respects plant provenance and the fact that plants do best in gardens most similar to where they were raised.

Garden clubs often hold plant sales as fundraisers. These sales are great places to meet fellow gardeners and are a source of unique, low-cost, hard-to-find specimens propagated by aficionados.

What to Look for When Shopping for Plants

What should you look for when you're shopping for plants? That depends on the kind of plant you're buying.

Herbaceous perennials, annuals, and biennials

Check for strong roots and shoots, and lots of them. The more shoots with healthy-looking leaves and stout stems, the better. While vigorous shoots usually signify strong roots, it's okay to pop a plant out of the pot to inspect them. You want to see healthy roots in the form of a root ball with no air pockets and definitely no pest infestations, like ants. If the roots of one plant of a group are fine, it's safe to assume the rest are too.

Plants growing in the same pot too long become root-bound, meaning the root ball has outgrown the container. Root-bound plants regularly wilt because there is more root mass absorbing water than potting mix holding water. Plants that repeatedly wilt are stressed and should be avoided. Vigorous growers like daylilies and ornamental grasses are often root-bound. This condition can be corrected by pruning the roots when you get home (more on this in the chapter on pruning). Even with pruning, there will be enough roots left to support the plant.

Garden center plants are regularly "up potted" into bigger pots before they become root-bound and reserved for sale until the roots are large enough to fill the new pot. Always check that you aren't paying for a gallon plant with quart-size roots. Remember, buying a plant means buying the roots, not just the foliage and the flowers. This is especially true with herbaceous perennials. Their shoots are seasonal, but their roots represent a long-term investment.

Woody trees and shrubs

You can't visually inspect all the roots on large shrubs and trees, but you can cast a critical eye on their shoots. Unlike herbaceous perennials that make a new set of shoots each year, woody plants have tops that last a lifetime, so their youthful form is important. Shop early in the year and choose deciduous trees and shrubs before they leaf out so you can inspect their branching.

Look for balanced structure and no broken branches. It's okay if some twigs have snapped, but not a large branch or major limb. Look for trees with U-shaped rather than

When you buy an herbaceous plant, look for vigorous shoots.

Look for healthy roots with no air pockets or pests.

Root-bound plants have been growing in the same pot too long.

Buy deciduous trees before they leaf out so you can inspect their structure.

Look for shrubs with a balanced form and healthy-looking stems and leaves.

V-shaped crotches. U-shaped crotches are strong because there is more wood to support a heavy limb. V-shaped crotches are weak and will be the first to break.

Plants define a garden's character, set its mood, and connect us with nature. Through the plants we select and nurture, we develop an intimate connection to our garden, improving our gardening instincts while feeding our passion for growing things. This connection can start even before a plant sprouts. Providing vast variety, low cost, and ease of shipment, seeds are a gardener's primal source for countless plants and the topic of our next chapter.

Large trees and shrubs should not be transported or planted when flowering. Even cautious handling is too disruptive when a tree is in bloom. Small shrubs in five-gallon pots or smaller can be handled gently and are okay to plant when flowering. The same is true for all herbaceous plants.

What's in a Name?

Botanical Latin is useful and fun once you know how it works. It's like a system of filters that narrows down a name so it can mean one plant and no other. Plants are grouped into families based on shared traits and evolutionary history. Plants within a family are grouped into genera that contain closely related plants. Within a genus, various species are distinct expressions of the genus characteristics. Species can be further subdivided into cultivars, names assigned by plant breeders to specific cultivated varieties. Botanical Latin plant names consist of the genus and the species, always italicized.

The words themselves tell a lot about the plant. For example, the genus for sunflower is *Helianthus*: *helio* = sun and *anthera* = flower. Species names tell more. Take *Echinacea purpurea*. That's purple coneflower. Or *Quercus alba*. *Quercus* means oak and *alba* means white, so that's a white oak. How about *Hydrangea macrophylla*? We know *hydrangea* since that is also the common name. Since *macro* = big and *phylla* = leaf, this is a bigleaf hydrangea. *Rosa multiflora*? That's right: multiflowered rose. Some gardeners take botanical Latin very seriously and practice perfect pronunciation, but the real joy is knowing your plants a little bit better.

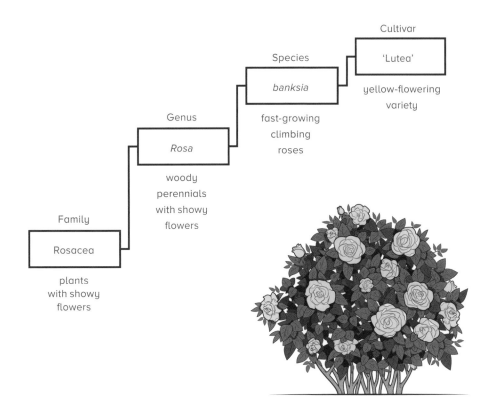

Cultivar

'Lutea'

yellow-flowering variety

Species

banksia

fast-growing climbing roses

Genus

Rosa

woody perennials with showy flowers

Family

Rosacea

plants with showy flowers

A simplified family tree for *Rosa banksia* 'Lutea' shows how its family, genus, species, and cultivar names narrow it down to a particular plant.

How to Read a Plant Tag

Plant tags bring people and plants together, linking the gardener's desire for the plant with the horticultural needs of the plant. What a plant wants is listed on its tag.

Common name Often related to historical references or regional monikers, common names are how nongardeners refer to plants in casual conversation. Think sunflower, spruce, and tomato. Common names sometimes match the botanical genus, as is the case for hosta (*Hosta* species) and hydrangea (*Hydrangea* species).

Scientific name Common names for plants have been passed down and altered through the years, so there may be several names for the same plant. To avoid confusion, all plants have a botanical Latin name, consisting of the genus and the species. For example, *Lagerstroemia indica* is the scientific name for crape myrtle. *Lagerstroemia* is the genus and *indica* is the species.

Cultivar name Plants that are cultivated varieties, hence "culti-vars," have an extra name, usually tied to breeding rights and patents. A cultivar name sometimes becomes so popular that it turns into the plant's accepted common name. An example is 'P.J.M.', a best-selling rhododendron.

Sun exposure How much sun the plant needs to perform best: full sun, part sun, or shade. Some tags reflect sun tolerances—for example, in the case of boxwoods, showing both full sun and shade.

Water needs The amount of soil moisture the plant prefers. "Wet," "moderately moist," and "dry between waterings" are the three common categories.

Size and spacing Size predictions, though based on genetics, are relatively subjective. Growing conditions, both general and specific, ultimately determine how big or small a plant grows. Sweet corn in full sun and fertile soil will reach fifteen feet tall, while the same plants in poor soil that is shaded will be puny. Spacing recommendations are based on size expectations, so adjust spacing according to how your growing conditions will affect plant size.

Hardiness zone The number of the coldest zone in which a perennial plant will survive an average winter. Plants with a hardiness zone number at or below the zone number of your garden are safe to plant. Those with a number higher than that should be considered annuals.

Soil preference The vast majority of garden plants call for moist, fertile, well-drained soil. If a tag indicates a plant's affinity for light and sandy or heavy and rich soil, take note and provide the right soil conditions.

Bloom season Never rely on precise dates or specific months for flowering indicated on tags. Bloom times vary from year to year and garden to garden. The best a tag can tell is the plant's genetic disposition to bloom early, mid, or late.

Pollinators and partners Some tags highlight a plant's attractiveness to pollinators, such as butterflies and bees, or make suggestions for companion plants that grow well and look good with this one.

**The tag tells you what the
plant wants and what it will provide.**

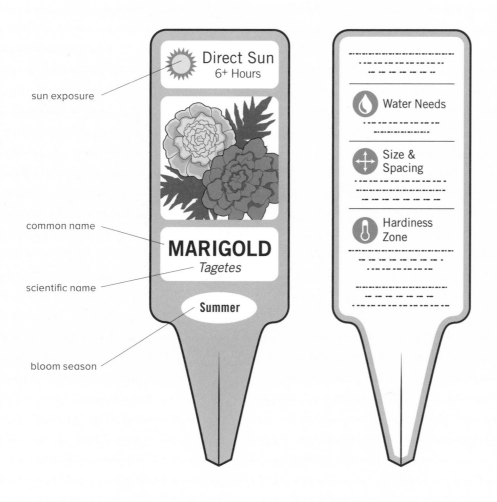

sun exposure

Direct Sun
6+ Hours

common name

MARIGOLD
Tagetes

scientific name

Summer

bloom season

Water Needs

Size &
Spacing

Hardiness
Zone

germination

Starting Plants from Seeds

All gardeners experience horticultural epiphanies—magical "aha" moments when how gardening works is suddenly and simply revealed. One such moment occurred for me when a renowned seed meister I met in Colorado casually assured me that "all seeds want to grow." We were standing in his backyard when he said it, surrounded by dozens of seed trays filled with seedlings in various stages of development arranged upon the ground. For him, making plants was matter-of-fact because he knew how plants—in this case seeds—work.

The mystery of a green thumb was revealed to be no mystery at all, because if all seeds want to grow, then by extension all plants want to grow too. Knowing this to be true is an important step toward learning how to enjoy gardening. I took that step in a garden on the outskirts of Denver and was never shy about trying to grow anything ever again, especially something from seed.

It's regrettable that most beginning gardeners shy away from starting seeds and instead buy ready-made plants from a store. There are so many great reasons to start with seeds, it seems the obvious choice once you know them. Then it's just a matter of gaining some basic knowledge about the step-by-step process of getting plants started from seeds.

There are two types of plant propagation: sexual, which is the sowing of seeds, and asexual, also called vegetative propagation, which is when we use a piece of a plant to make a new plant. The latter is discussed in a later chapter.

You can find seeds in hardware stores, garden centers, and gift shops, buy them from online retailers, or collect them yourself from private gardens and in the wild.

Why Start Plants from Seeds?

The selection of ready-made plants available at even the best garden stores is just the tip of the botanical iceberg. Plant breeders grow only what they know will make a profit, leaving a tremendous variety of plants available only from seed. Happily, seeds are inexpensive—just a few dollars for a packet that will produce twenty, thirty, forty, or more plants.

Propagating from seed also ensures genetic diversity. This may be desirable when propagating plants susceptible to certain diseases because these inherited weaknesses can be mitigated over time through breeding. Genetic diversity also leads to new and exciting plant attributes such as unusual flower colors or foliage patterns.

Though there may be an occasional regret, starting seeds is fun if you approach it as an inexpensive adventure. When the seeds succeed, the time invested becomes a small price to pay for a vast batch of new plants. Besides, how many people get to say they've known their plants from the very beginning, including the old oak tree left as a legacy for their great-grandchildren?

Seeds are inexpensive, and many plants are available only from seed.

How to Store Seeds

The "Packed for" and "Sell by" dates on seed packets indicate the year of optimal viability in which to sow those seeds. While it's always best to use fresh seeds, you don't necessarily have to throw away seeds past these dates. Viability does diminish over time, but a certain percentage of old seeds will germinate. I like to say, "The softer the seed, the sooner it should be sown." Soft seeds include those for grasses and annuals. Hard seeds, like those of many native perennials, remain viable for decades.

Store seeds in a consistently cool, dry place out of direct sunlight, like a cold closet or unheated basement. Paper bags and envelopes are fine, but an airtight container such as a sealed mason jar or spice canister keeps seeds safe from pests and allows you to store them in the refrigerator. For long-term storage of two years or more, put the container in the freezer. Not all seeds store well. Seeds like those of carrots and onions spoil rapidly and must be frozen. Make sure the seeds are dry before you store them. Moist seeds can rot or get freezer burn.

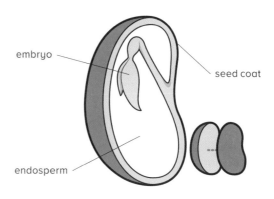

A seed is a plant-in-waiting.

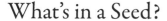

A small seed buried too deep won't have enough endosperm energy to get out of the ground, and a big seed planted not deep enough might flop over. The rule of thumb is to use the size of a seed to determine planting depth and never to bury a seed deeper than three times its longest dimension.

What's in a Seed?

Simply put, a seed is a plant waiting to be. Every viable seed has a protoplant, called an embryo, lying dormant inside it. The embryo becomes the seedling. It has all the necessary parts of a complete plant: root, stem, and leaves, ready to activate when the conditions of germination are met.

There's also something called endosperm. That's the meat of the seed, the bit of bean we bite into. Endosperm is food for us and food for the embryo. Some seeds are big because the embryo needs a lot of food to get started. Some are tiny because the embryo needs less. Every seed needs just enough food energy to initiate growth of the radicle (Latin for "small root") into the soil and extend the stem out of the ground.

The radicle is a plant's first root. It explores the soil and starts to absorb water and nutrients as it grows. While that happens, the embryo's shoot rises out of the ground and opens leaflike structures called cotyledons. These are part of the seed and provide enough nourishment to last until the first true leaves are formed. The leaves turn green and the photosynthesis factories (chloroplasts) kick in. As it makes more roots, the plant can absorb more water and nutrients from the soil. These nutrients are then used to make more shoots and leaves. The additional leaves in turn photosynthesize more food to make more roots, and so on. This balanced cycle between the roots and the shoots is the hallmark of every healthy plant grown in the ground.

There is, however, one obstacle to all this growth: the seed coat. The seed coat protects the embryo inside, allowing for handling and transport of the plant-to-be, whether tucked in a packet for sale, wedged in the beak of a bird, or whipping across a field on the wind. For a seed to germinate, its protective case, the seed coat, must be compromised. The tougher the coat, the more difficult that task, which brings us to the topic of germination.

What a Seed Needs to Germinate

The seed meister who told me, "All seeds want to grow," went on to say, "Provide them with what they need to get started and nature will do the rest." Fortunately, what seeds need to sprout is pretty simple: ample water, adequate oxygen, and optimal temperature. Most seeds germinate in darkness, but some, like lettuce and petunias, need light to germinate, and some seeds need special treatment of the seed coat.

Water swells the seed and initiates growth. No water = no swelling = no seedling. That's why when seeding a lawn, it's best to do it during a rainy season and be prepared to water it every day—sometimes twice a day in hot weather—for the first month. If a seed sprouts and then dries out, it will die.

Oxygen must also be present, in the soil and in the air, for the seedling to grow. Plants "breathe" carbon dioxide during photosynthesis, but they need oxygen to fuel growth. This is called respiration. Everything alive on earth respires: people, plants, and animals.

Temperature means the temperature of the soil, not the air. Most seeds germinate when the soil reaches 75 to 85 degrees F. That's why gardeners use heating mats to start seeds inside chilly greenhouses or lay biodegradable black fabric or paper on vegetable rows to absorb heat from the sun and warm the soil.

Some seeds need help breaking out of the seed coat in order to germinate. Soft coats, such as those of winter rye and marigold seeds, pose no problem. They germinate easily when wet and basic conditions are met. It's the sturdy seed coats of delphinium, hibiscus, castor bean, and many

Seeds in Fruits or Cones

Seed-bearing plants are classified as either angiosperms or gymnosperms, according to how they hold their seeds. Angiosperms sport fruit and gymnosperms carry cones. Unlike these, ferns and mosses propagate by way of spores instead of seeds.

The term *angiosperm* is based on the Greek words *angion* = vessel and *sperma* = seed. Angiosperms are plants with seeds formed inside containers called fruits. Think tomatoes, apples, pumpkins, and pears. The majority of all landscape and crop plants are angiosperms.

Gymnosperm is based on the Greek *gymno* = naked and *sperma* = seed, so gymnosperms are plants that form seeds in open spaces, most commonly on cones. Thus, all conifers are gymnosperms. This includes pine, spruce, fir, cedar, and yew trees, as well as cycads, palmlike plants found in subtropical and tropical regions of the world. The gingko, a popular street tree, is also a gymnosperm.

All gymnosperms are descended from plants that grew 400 million years ago, during the Paleozoic Era. Angiosperms evolved much later, about 145 million years ago.

more that require some coaxing to break their seal. There are two ways this happens. The first and more common way, called cold stratification, is when a seed experiences a period of cold, 40 degrees F or less, for several weeks. This can take place naturally in the ground over the winter or in a plastic bag in the refrigerator during any season.

The key to stratification is that the seed gets cold and stays cold. When it warms up it wakes up, either the following spring or when the gardener removes the seed from the fridge and sows it, indoors or out. Why does it work like this? It's a matter of survival. Consider the thousands of seeds dispersed by trees late in the season. If they all

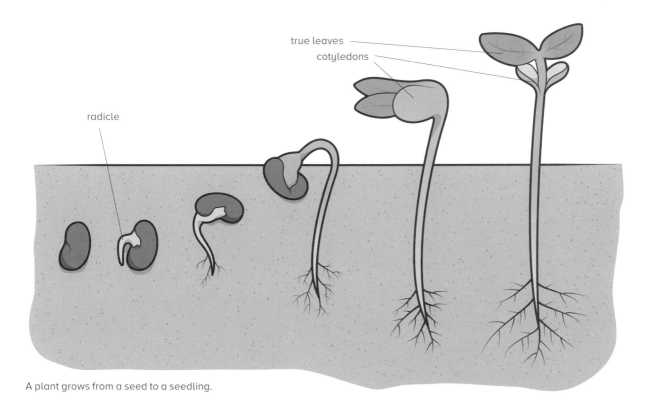

true leaves

cotyledons

radicle

A plant grows from a seed to a seedling.

germinated when they hit the ground, there wouldn't be enough time for them to grow strong enough to survive the winter. So instead, the seeds remain dormant through summer and fall. After they are stratified over winter they germinate the following spring, when they have a complete growing season to make strong roots and shoots before winter sets in again.

The other way plant seeds delay germination, sometimes for decades, is by requiring scarification, a process by which the seed coat is physically damaged or "scarred" so that water can infiltrate to the embryo. Getting roughed over by sand particles underground is often enough, but many seeds pass through birds that eat the fruit and expel the seed with their poop. That's an experience that would scar anyone.

There are even tougher seeds that need nothing less than a full-blown forest fire to compromise their coat. For example, the seeds of the bristlecone pine of mountainous western North America may lie on the ground for decades but never germinate. Most get eaten by foragers, but many

Gardener's Glossary

Angiosperms form flowers and produce seeds inside of fruits.

Gymnosperms do not form flowers, and they produce seeds in open spaces, like a cone.

Cold stratification is the process of subjecting seeds to a period of cold conditions to break their dormancy.

Scarification is the weakening or altering of the coat of a seed to encourage germination.

Hardening off is the gradual acclimation of indoor plants to outdoor conditions.

A **cold frame** is a transparent-roofed enclosure built low to the ground, used to protect plants from adverse weather.

remain on the forest floor, dormant until the day there's fire on the mountain. The trees are burned to cinders and ash, which is a perfect soil amendment for the bumper crop of baby pine trees that blankets the slopes after the next cycle of rain.

Plant Seeds That Need Stratification

black-eyed Susan
bleeding heart
columbine
coneflower
clematis
cranesbill
daylily
delphinium
dianthus
lavender
pansy/violet
peony
phlox
rose
salvia
snapdragon
sweet pea

Plant Seeds That Need Scarification

angel's trumpet
canna
castor bean
false indigo
hollyhock
mallow
moonflower
morning glory
nasturtium

How to Scarify Seeds

Scarification can be done manually with a piece of sandpaper, the nick of a knife, or a short bath in vinegar. A simple compromise of the coat to allow moisture in is all that's needed.

- If a seed is large enough to hold, you can use 120-grit sandpaper and rub the seed until the outer coating is dull but not to the point of pitting or cracking the seed.

- You can nick a seed that's large enough to hold by using a nail clipper or a knife. Make as shallow a cut as you can to allow water inside the seed coat.

- If you want to scarify a bunch of seeds all at once, make a solution of one part apple cider vinegar to four parts warm water and pour the vinegar solution over the seeds in a glass jar. There should be twice as much solution as seeds. Let the seeds soak for twelve hours and rinse them before planting.

Be sure to plant seeds immediately after you scarify them. And never scarify a seed that doesn't need it. You can kill it.

You can scarify seeds with a sharp knife or sandpaper.

Starting Seeds Indoors

Should you sow seeds indoors or outdoors? The answer depends on the type of seeds being started and your available resources of time, effort, equipment, and work space. In general, plants with delicate seedlings or that take longer to mature from seed should be started indoors. Plants with seeds that germinate quickly or don't transplant should be sown outside in the garden.

It's good to remember that there's a time commitment to consider when starting seeds, especially if you sow them indoors under lights. Seeds become seedlings, which are basically baby plants, and they require patience and consistent care. Seeds can also experience a failure rate not everyone is willing to tolerate. There is nothing more disheartening than waking one day to find your seedlings flopped over dead, victims of the dreaded damping off, a fungal disease to which all seedlings are susceptible.

The benefit of starting seeds indoors is to get a jump on the season. In northern latitudes that have short summers, starting plants indoors in late winter can add a month or two to their growing season. This applies especially to annual vegetables that require a long growing season to produce good fruit, such as tomatoes, eggplants, and peppers. Starting seeds indoors is also a neat way to have annual flowers like pansies, petunias, and impatiens already big and blooming in early spring.

Ten Plants to Start Indoors
celery
eggplant
peppers
tomatoes
begonias
delphiniums
geraniums
impatiens
lupines
primroses
salvia

The Dreaded Damping Off

A general term for several fungal diseases, damping off is easy to recognize as seedling stems rot at the soil line and flop over. Overcrowding of seedlings is a primary contributor when dampness and poor air circulation make conditions rife with fungi. Once a plant falls prey, it is finished. Preventive measures, such as ensuring good air circulation, prudent watering, using sterile soilless mix, and keeping tools and equipment sanitized help prevent this menace to seedlings indoors or out.

Damping off causes seedlings to flop over dead.

How to Determine the Viability of Old Seeds

Sometimes we buy more seeds than we need. This is especially true when the seed catalogs arrive in the wintertime and our passion for plants gets the better of us. Fortunately, there is an easy way to determine if old seeds are viable using only a dinner plate, a couple of paper towels, and plastic wrap. This method works best with large, easier-to-handle seeds, but you can try smaller seeds if you like to work with tweezers.

1. Place a paper towel on an old dinner plate and wet the paper towel.

2. Neatly place seeds on the plate in a grid pattern, leaving a half inch to an inch between seeds.

3. Place a paper towel over the seeds and wet the paper towel.

4. Wrap the plate in plastic wrap and lightly seal.

5. Set the wrapped seedling plate by a sunny window. Wait three to five days. Lift the plastic wrap and check the seedlings. If just a few show signs of a root radicle, or if there is no activity, reseal the plastic wrap and put the plate back by the window. Wait two to three more days.

6. Lift the plastic wrap and check the seedlings again. If more, or most, or some seeds now show a root radicle, these are your winners. Dismantle the wrapping and plant these seeds right away in their own cell or peat pellet. If there is still nothing happening, wet the paper towel some more, seal the plate, and put it by the window for another five to seven days. Still nothing? Those seeds are probably not viable. You can let them sit in the sun another week just in case or toss them in the compost pile and try some others.

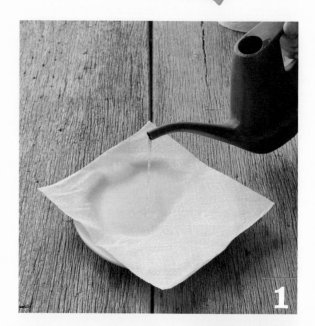

Step 1: Prepare the medium

To start seeds indoors, use seed trays, twelve by sixteen inches or smaller and at least three inches deep. They should have drainage holes or slits to allow water to pass though the bottom. The best trays have a bottom mesh built right in. There are fancy seed trays made of wood, and practical plastic types. Ground cover flats from buying pachysandra or vinca at a nursery can be reused to start seeds. Stop in at your local garden center and ask if they have any surplus trays lying around. If they know you and you're nice, they'll give you all you need.

Don't start seeds in cell pack trays, or worse yet, those little compressed discs of peat, called pellets, that expand with water. Savvy gardeners use trays because they never know if every seed will germinate. To place a single seed in a cell or peat pellet commits that bit of space and soil to the viability of a seed that can't be guaranteed. Some seeds work and some don't, so it's safer to scatter them in a tray and let whatever germinates germinate.

Fill your seed tray with a seed-starting mix, basically a fifty-fifty blend of sphagnum peat moss and perlite. The peat moss retains moisture and the perlite provides proper drainage, both important characteristics that keep seedlings happy as they develop in a tray. Limestone and a wetting agent are occasionally added to seed-starting mixes. Limestone neutralizes the acidity of the peat moss, while a wetting agent helps the peat more effectively absorb water so delicate seedlings won't wilt and die. A sixteen-quart bag of store-bought seed-starting mix will fill two or three trays. If you plan to start more seeds than that, save money by making your own mix. I use peat moss (or coir), perlite, and horticultural grade sand (which has rounded grains that won't clump together). All are available at garden centers and online.

You can make your own seed-starting mix to save money, using peat moss (or coir), perlite, and sand.

Coir, or coconut fiber, is a substitute for peat moss that is more sustainable. Peat moss is a naturally occuring product mined from ancient peat bogs. Technically it's a renewable resource, but on a geologic timeline—it takes millions of years to make the stuff. It takes a lot less time to grow a coconut than it does to form an ancient peat bog, but you need a lot of coconuts.

Step 2: Sow the seeds and provide light and water

Sow seeds by scattering them on the surface of the seed-starting mix. If they're touching soil, they're good to go. If the seeds are really small, such as with many wild-flower mixes, the trick is to shake the seeds into a cup of sand, stir it, and sprinkle the sand on the soil. This will distribute the seeds evenly. Lightly cover the seeds with the mix by gently raking the surface with your fingertips.

You will need to provide either natural light or grow lights to help the seeds germinate and the newly sprouted leaves photosynthesize. The natural light on a windowsill or in a greenhouse is best because it has all the wavelengths of light needed for optimal growth. If the natural light is limited, as in a basement or a garage, special grow lights should be suspended over the trays.

Keep the seed mix moist until germination but don't overdo it. It should never get soggy. Spritz the surface every few days with a light mist from a spray bottle and keep the soil from drying out with a clear plastic cover or kitchen plastic wrap tented over the top of the tray.

The best way to keep seed-starting mix moist is with a light mist.

Sow seeds by scattering them on the soil.

Keep the soil from drying out by tenting plastic wrap over the tray.

Step 3: Monitor the seedlings

It's vital that the seedlings not dry out at any time after germination. When young they are too delicate to survive drought, so continue to monitor the moisture of the mix. Keep on spritzing but don't saturate the soil. Baby roots don't like that.

When the seedlings are an inch or two tall, remove the cover. They are more likely to thrive with good air circulation. That's also the time to switch from misting to bottom watering. The seedlings are still too delicate to water directly from a can or hose, but they need more moisture than misting provides. Set the seed tray on a sheet tray and fill it with water. The water will wick through the drainage holes and keep the soil mix moist.

Switch to bottom watering when the seedlings are an inch or two tall.

Step 4: Prick out to select the strongest seedlings

Pricking out is nothing more than gently removing seedlings from the seed tray to be "potted on" and given more room to grow. Seedlings are ready to prick out when they have formed one or two sets of true leaves. Some will be stronger and healthier than others because as the seedlings fill the tray they start to compete for water and nutrients. Their roots get crowded, especially in spots where a lot of seeds landed and germinated side by side. At this stage, the gardener must select the strongest of the brood so each baby plant has a fighting chance.

Prick out with a pencil, a chopstick, or even a plant tag. The novice gardener's first inclination is to be super careful and treat each seedling as if it were a delicate living creature wholly dependent upon the benevolence of a greater being. Oh wait, it is, and that greater being is you! But plants are tougher than we think, even little seedlings.

Prick out seedlings using a pencil, a chopstick, or even a plant tag.

Don't be afraid to pull the seedlings apart to inspect their roots and shoots. It gets easier as you go, and after you prick out several dozen seedlings from a single tray, with neck and shoulders beginning to ache, it's tempting to speed things up. This may damage a few, but that's fine. There's a moment in every gardener's evolution when the loss of a plant is no longer tragic. Plants die. Sometimes we kill them, sometimes by mistake, sometimes on purpose. Thanks to propagation, we can always make more.

Step 5: Pot on

Immediately after pricking out, we pot on—meaning we transfer each tiny seedling to its own cell or small pot where it will continue to grow. Plant each seedling so its roots are buried completely and the stem stands upright on its own. Use soilless potting mix with a little compost or a sprinkle of organic granular fertilizer. This provides a fertility boost so the baby plants keep making more roots and shoots.

Always pot on, or up-pot, in stages: seed tray to cell pack or two-inch pot, two-inch pot to four-inch pot, four-inch pot to six-inch pot, and so on. *Do not* skip a step thinking to save time. The plants must have enough root mass to absorb the amount of moisture held by the potting mix in the next pot. If there aren't enough roots to use the water, the result will be a soggy mess that at best stunts the plants and at worst kills them.

It *is* okay to plant a lot of small fast-growing annual flowers in a large container knowing that they will quickly fill in. In this case, though, make sure the potting mix stays moist but not soggy.

Pot on to give each seedling more room to grow.

Step 6: Harden off

Hardening off is acclimating seedlings to live outdoors. This is especially important if the seedlings were started indoors under lights, but it's also necessary for seedlings started in a greenhouse. Any indoor plant must be prepared before it's moved out to the garden, and it's up to the gardener to toughen 'em up. This takes time because the trick is to gradually expose the plants to outside elements. A cold frame is a great tool to make hardening off easier.

The best kind of day to take your seedlings outside is a cool, cloudy one. If it's sunny, be sure to set the plants in the shade. Direct sunlight on that first foray will fry them for sure. Leave them outside all day but bring them in overnight or close the cold frame those first few times, and whenever frost threatens. In three weeks' time they will

A cold frame makes it easier to harden off seedlings by gradually exposing them to the outside elements.

do fine in their preferred sun exposure. Once all threat of frost has passed they can be planted directly into the ground, as described in the next chapter.

When starting seeds indoors during the growing season, harden off your seedlings while they are still in trays. It's easier because there are fewer things to move in and out of the house, and it separates the stronger seedlings from the weaklings before you go to the trouble of pricking out and potting on. You still must prick out and pot on at least one step before planting the seedlings out in the garden, however.

Starting Seeds Outdoors

It's better to start herbaceous perennials outside, unless they are from a climate much milder than yours. Perennial seedlings, especially those of native plants, respond best when exposed to the whims of the weather, resulting in hardier mature specimens that thrive with minimal maintenance. Direct sowing outdoors is also the preferred method for difficult-to-transplant or fast-maturing edible plants like carrots and lettuce, respectively.

Decide whether to sow the seeds directly in the ground or in trays based on the type and quantity of plants you want to grow and the time you can commit to their care. Direct sowing is less labor intensive, but there may be more failures due to weather and pests. Trays provide greater control. The chances of success increase when you use a seed-starting mix and when you can manage exposure to sun and moisture by moving seedlings in and out of a cold frame. Seedlings left exposed to the elements won't

Ten Plants to Start Outdoors

basil
butterfly bush
lettuce
morning glory
nasturtium
native wildflowers
radishes
St. John's wort
sweet pea
zinnia

fertilizer and compost, then rake the surface smooth. Plant in rows or hills spaced as instructed on the seed packet, and label what you plant. When sowing seeds between existing plantings, always mark the spot with a stake and a label. Supplement rainfall with a gentle shower from a hose or watering can, being careful to not wash away the seeds or drown the seedlings as they emerge.

need hardening off, which saves time and effort, but they could be damaged by an unexpected cold snap, heat wave, or drought.

Direct sowing can be done at any time of year as long as the soil isn't frozen or muddy. Seeds sown in early spring will germinate and establish then. Seeds sown in autumn will overwinter and emerge as growing conditions develop the following spring. Summer sowing is best for fast-growing herbs or to set the stage for fall crops and flowers.

Preparation of the seedbed is the most important step in direct sowing. Loosen the soil, break up clumps, and clear away debris like sticks and stones. Amend with organic

Long before I became a professional gardener, I had heard about saving, storing, and exchanging seeds. Inspired by the ethical, even moral, act of sowing a saved rather than a store-bought seed, I've enjoyed successes and suffered some failures. Faith in a seed, be it an heirloom tomato passed down through the generations or a native plant charged with cultural heritage, is something all gardeners share. The Colorado seed meister had filing cabinets filled with thousands of native perennial seeds collected over the years. Those seeds were a symptom of his plantsman's passion, and they signaled to me the belief that everything—and everyone, new gardeners included—can grow into something extraordinary, however humble the origin.

planting and mulching

Establishing Plants the Right Way

The first time I ever planted something was when I was on a landscaping crew during college. My foreman showed me how to do it fast: dig a hole, pop the plant out of the pot, stuff the plant into the ground, fill the hole, stomp the soil, move on to the next one. When years later I learned how to plant as a gardener, I realized the difference between landscapers and gardeners. While the actions are similar, the intentions are very different. When landscapers plant something, their job is done. When gardeners plant something, it's just the beginning. They assume responsibility for that plant, and proper planting and mulching assures it gets off to a healthy start, setting the stage for the season, years, or generations to come.

Prepare the soil before you bring the plants home.

Step 1

Preparing a Garden Bed

Preparing the ground for planting before you bring plants home from the nursery saves time on planting day and ensures the plants go into the ground without delay. The added effort of preparing the soil properly so as to nurture the plant roots is the best insurance for a successful start.

To prepare a new bed

Preparing a new bed requires clearing the area, turning the soil, and adding desired amendments based on the results of a soil test. For edibles, select a sunny site, because most need all-day sun to produce the best fruit.

Step 1 Clear the area of weeds, lawn, or whatever is in that spot, growing or not. Grub down to bare ground with a hoe or a shovel, scraping off the top two to three inches of plant roots and soil. Power equipment like a sod cutter is a labor saver for large-scale projects involving areas more than ten feet square. Shake the soil from the clods of turf or weed roots back onto the new bed and toss the plants on the compost pile.

Step 2 Turn the soil by digging down twelve to eighteen inches or more deep with a garden fork or rototiller to eliminate soil compaction. Roots spread easily through loose soil, so the deeper you dig the better the root run for your new plants. Do this just to establish the bed and never again, allowing the soil food web to rebuild.

Step 2

Step 3

Step 3 Add amendments such as compost, organic fertilizers (more on these in the next chapter), or ingredients like sand to improve drainage or peat to retain moisture. Spread them on the surface and mix them in by turning the soil with a garden fork or bow rake. This is the best opportunity you will have to mix improving ingredients into the soil, so add what you can now.

Raised beds, either mounded on the ground or in boxes, are an alternative that allows roots to run easily and the soil to warm up sooner in the spring, initiating earlier growth. Planters filled with good garden soil are best for growing edibles on a terrace, deck, or rooftop because they are self-contained and easy to manage.

To prepare an existing bed

To get an existing bed ready for planting, first rake away any mulch. Scoop up and place the mulch in a bucket or wheelbarrow or on a tarp until planting is completed so it doesn't find its way into the planting hole, where it might form large air pockets that roots can't grow through. Then top-dress the planting area by spreading a layer of compost a half inch deep over the soil. The compost will work its way into the soil when you dig the hole and will help promote root growth.

How to Make New Garden Beds Without Digging or Tilling

Here are two no-dig, no-till techniques to prepare new garden beds.

Raised bed Simply dump a 60/40 blend of topsoil and compost directly on the ground. Rake it smooth into a low mound at least eighteen inches high and plant directly into the fresh mix. The depth of the soil will smother lawn or weeds underneath it. In tight spots, raised beds should be contained with structures made of wood, stone, or bricks.

Lasagna gardening Rather than turning completed compost into existing soil where a new bed is wanted, spread layers of compostables on the ground and leave them to biodegrade in place. Start with a layer of browns, like newsprint or cardboard, and alternate layers of greens, like lawn clippings and manure, and more browns, like dried leaves and straw. Add enough layers to build a low mound. In several months, once the lasagna has settled to half its height, plant directly into the mound and treat it like a regular garden bed.

Tools for Digging, Spreading, and Raking

Using the right tool for the job is as important in gardening as it is for everything else. For digging and raking, lighter is best, so choose fiberglass over wood handles when available. Check for connecting welds where the handle meets the tool, avoiding rivets and screws.

A **groundbreaker spade** has a pointed metal blade on a long handle and is the perfect tool to break new ground.

A **garden spade** consists of a long handle and a semi-flat blade, and is designed for preparing beds and turning the soil. Providing the leverage needed to dig a deep hole or scoop topsoil from a pile, this shovel is practical and practically ubiquitous in every garden.

A **garden fork** has four flat, stiff tines attached to a stout handle. Use it to turn a bed, break up clods, and loosen soil for planting.

A **bow rake** has an eighteen-inch-wide business end with fourteen to sixteen stiff, curved tines. It effectively spreads soil, levels disturbed soil, and mixes in amendments with a brisk back-and-forth action.

A **soft rake** has a fan of flexible tines. Use it to complete the job by finely leveling loose soil in preparation for plants or mulch. It's also perfect to sweep soil, mulch, or clippings from lawns.

A **potato hoe** is a three- or four-clawed mini-rake. It works well when breaking up clods of soil or smoothing narrow areas between plants.

When to Plant

A harried gardener might say the best time to plant is whenever there is time to do it, but spring is the absolutely best time to plant anything. This timing gives perennial plants an entire growing season to establish, and annuals more time to complete their life cycle. However, exceptions can be made

Tools for digging include a groundbreaker spade (left), a garden fork (center), and a garden spade (right).

Tools for loosening soil, spreading, and raking include a bow rake (left), a soft rake (center), and a potato hoe (right).

to stretch the planting season based on the type of plant going into the ground. Summer is the worst time, unless you are willing to stay a slave to the watering can or hose.

Woodies (trees and shrubs) Plant in early spring before bud break or late fall after leaf drop. Large specimens have a better survival rate if planted when dormant.

Herbaceous perennials Spring planting is best, but early autumn is fine if daytime temperatures stay above freezing and the plants have time to grow more roots before frost sets in.

Annuals Plant in late spring, after the last frost. However, there are many annual flowers and edibles that can survive a frost. These plants can go into the

Frost-Tolerant Annuals

cabbage

calendula

carrot

dianthus

dusty miller

forget-me-not

kale

pansy

parsley

radish

ranunculus

Swiss chard

viola

Gardener's Glossary

A **root ball** is a compact mass of roots and soil that accompanies a plant to be planted or transplanted.

A **root-bound** plant has a root ball that has outgrown its container.

The **root flare** is the part of a tree where the trunk widens just above the soil line and roots emerge.

Bare-root plants are dormant trees, shrubs, and herbaceous perennials sold in late winter without any soil around their roots.

To **backfill** is to use the soil you removed to fill a planting hole. **Backfill** is also the term for the soil you removed.

Mulch is material spread on the ground around plants to conserve soil moisture and keep down weeds.

Transplanting is digging up and moving a plant from one spot to another in the garden.

ground weeks sooner and are especially useful for early spring pots or in gardens where winters are mild.

Bulbs Plant in late fall, after the first frost. The danger comes from planting too early. If warm weather returns, the bulbs may break dormancy and emerge from the ground prematurely. Reputable mail-order sources won't ship bulbs until the time is right.

Planting the Right Way

No matter what you plant, you follow the same basic steps. However, there are some variations based on how the plants are packaged for sale—in containers, balled and burlapped, or bare root.

Container-grown plants

Most plants are sold in plastic pots. Plants raised in containers tend to have compact roots, so the essential task with them is to prepare the root ball for life in the open ground. This applies to plants in pots of all sizes, from a single quart to seven gallons or larger. Small plants in three- or four-inch pots, and plugs are the exceptions. These are easily planted in beds properly prepared ahead of time simply by scooping the soil aside with your hands and pressing them into the ground.

Step 1 Remove the container. Knock a few times on the sides of the pot with the heel of your hand, then tip the container on its side and shake the plant free. Hold the pot in one hand and catch the root ball with the other hand. If that doesn't do it, use hand pruners to make two or three cuts down the side of the pot and peel it open.

Step 2 Inspect the roots. Check for soft, rotted sections and cut them out. Tease out some roots to give the root ball a shaggy surface. This creates better contact with the soil inside the hole. If the plant is root-bound, slice vertically along the sides of the root ball every few inches with a knife or pruner blade. Sliced roots will respond by dividing at growth points, ultimately increasing root mass.

Most plants are sold in plastic pots and need to have the root ball prepared for life in the open ground.

Step 1

Step 2

Step 3

Step 4

Step 5

Step 4 Position the plant, making sure it is standing straight with its best side facing where it will be seen. Slowly fill the planting hole with water, completely soaking the root ball without breaking it apart. Wait for the water to drain.

Step 5 Use the soil you removed to fill the hole, covering the bottom half of the root ball. This is called backfilling and that soil is called backfill. *Do not* compact the soil with your hands or feet. Add water to settle the soil and repeat the process until the soil filling the hole is level with the ground around it.

Use a length of string to bind unruly shoots that get in the way of accessing the planting hole when you are backfilling and watering.

Step 3 Dig a hole four to eight inches wider than the root ball and deep enough so the top of the root ball is level with the surface of the soil when you slip it into the ground. If the planting bed was not prepared ahead of time, make the hole two or three times as wide as the root ball to encourage the roots to spread into the surrounding soil.

Step 6

Step 7

Step 6 Make a raised bank, or berm, two to four inches high in a ring around the buried root ball. This will direct water to the root zone when it rains and when you water. Fill the water ring, allowing the water to soak in slowly. Reshape the berm if it collapses.

Step 7 Apply a layer of mulch two to three inches thick to cover the root zone and the water ring. Do not cover the crown of herbaceous plants (the area where the stem joins the root) or let the mulch touch the stems or trunks of woody plants. Mulch in direct contact with plant parts can cause rot and fungal diseases. Water the mulched area one last time and you're done.

Opinions differ among professional gardeners about the benefit of adding compost or organic fertilizer to the backfill. Some say this gets nutrients close to the roots and promotes root growth. Some warn that if conditions in the planting hole are too favorable, roots won't spread into the surrounding soil. They're both right. If the surrounding soil is exceptionally poor, roots won't leave a fertile hole, but if the ground nearby is good, extra nutrients around the roots help plants start strong.

Field-grown trees and shrubs arrive at the planting site balled and burlapped.

Balled-and-burlapped plants

Large field-grown trees and shrubs come balled in burlap. Nursery workers excavate a large root ball either by hand or with a tree spade, then wrap it in burlap and tie it tight so it can be lifted safely out of the ground for transport.

Step 1 Inspect the root ball and find the root flare of the tree or shrub to determine proper planting depth. On most trees, the root flare is two to four inches below the top of the root ball. The base of this flare must be at or slightly above ground level when the tree or shrub is planted.

When digging a large hole in a lawn, set a square of burlap or a tarp on the ground and pile the soil on top of that so it's easier to scoop up later.

Step 1

Step 2

Step 2 Dig a hole two to three times wider than the root ball. The extra width is needed so you can work inside the hole during step 5. Check the depth as you dig, using a measuring stick or tape. Check often so you do not dig too deep.

Step 3 Lower the plant into the hole, double-checking that the depth is correct. If you do dig the hole too deep, put back enough soil so the root flare will be two or three inches above grade. This allows for settling. With the tree or shrub in the hole, carefully turn it so the best side (the "face") is on view, and make sure it is standing straight when seen from all angles.

Step 3

Step 4

Step 5

Step 6

Step 7

Step 4 If including soil amendments, add them to the pile of backfill now. Backfill around the root ball a third of the way up to hold it in place. Use a soft stream of water to settle the soil.

Step 5 Remove any wire or twine and all the burlap from the top portion of the root ball. Work down as far as possible. Bolt cutters make short work of wire, and a utility knife can handle the burlap and any twine. Double-check

again the depth of the root flare, being careful not to break the root ball apart.

Step 6 Keep backfilling and watering until the soil is fully settled and level with the surface of the ground around the plant. *Do not* compact the soil with your feet. Make a small berm two to four inches high in a ring around the root ball. This directs water to the root zone when it rains and when you water.

Planting Trees at the Right Level

If a tree is planted too deep, meristematic tissue in the buried trunk will develop into roots that cross over and strangle the root flares that support the plant. This is detrimental for the tree because if the phloem is blocked, downward flow stops. The roots will weaken and die, and in time the tree will too.

Trees should not look like telephone poles. A properly planted tree has root flares visible on the surface level.

A tree that looks like a telephone pole (left) has been planted too deep. Root flares should be visible on the surface level (right).

Step 7 Water again to settle the soil inside the water ring, and reshape the berm if it collapses. Fill the ring with water one last time and let it seep slowly into the soil. Then apply a layer of mulch two to three inches thick covering the root zone and the water ring. Don't let any mulch touch the trunk of a tree or the stems of a shrub. Mulch in direct contact with plant parts can cause rot and fungal diseases.

Many tree professionals advise removing *all* wire, twine, and burlap from the entire root ball. A pro with years of experience and the right equipment can remove it all from even the largest trees, but home gardeners should follow these steps instead. While removing all the packaging material is certainly preferable, if the root ball breaks apart during planting, the plant will most likely die. To avoid this possibility, remove packaging materials from the root ball only after it is in the planting hole, which will mean you can remove the materials only from the top portion. Over time any remaining twine and burlap will rot, and the bottom wire will rust away. Because the majority of roots grow out of the top portion of the root ball, the danger of root growth being impeded by the wire is limited from the start.

Step 1

Step 2

Bare-root plants

Mail-order plants are often sold bare root to lower shipping costs. Dug in the winter and stored in root cellars, they are shipped only in early spring while dormant. Roses and other shrubs are often sold bare root, as are many herbaceous perennials and even large trees. The key concern when buying bare root is never to let the roots dry out. If they do, the plant will die.

Step 1 Before planting, soak the roots for at least twenty-four hours in a bucket of water placed in a cool, shady spot indoors or out. Use lukewarm water and submerge just the roots, not the trunk or stems.

Step 3

How to Plant Bulbs

Plant bulbs in masses. More is better when it comes to bulbs. My two design rules for including bulbs are to plant twice as many as you think you need and to space them randomly. I simply toss them on the ground and plant them where they land.

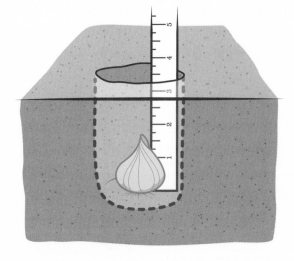

Plant a bulb twice as deep as it is wide.

The fast way to plant a lot of bulbs is to use an auger on a drill. A nursery spade with proper leverage also works well. As a general rule, plant twice as deep as the bulb is wide.

Add a high potassium or phosphorus fertilizer to the planting hole to establish strong roots. After filling in with soil, cover bulb plantings with buried chicken wire or add a layer of sharp gravel just below the surface of each planting hole to discourage squirrels and other critters.

Step 4

Step 2 An advantage of bare-root plants is the opportunity to closely inspect and prune the roots. Cut off roots growing inward and keep the roots that spread outward. Remove just a few, and handle the young, small roots carefully so as not to damage them.

Step 3 Dig a hole wide enough so the roots can be spread out and deep enough so the root flare is level with the ground. Find the flare at the point where the bark on the main stem changes. Look for a knot or bulge where the roots transition from the main stem.

Step 4 Add soil amendments, like compost or organic fertilizer, to the pile of soil you dug from the hole. Mound some soil at the bottom of the hole and place the plant on top of the mound, spreading its roots out over it. Double-check that the root flare is level with the ground.

Step 5

Step 6

Step 5 Break up any clods of soil and backfill the hole halfway. Add water to settle the soil around the roots, repeating the process multiple times until the roots are completely buried and air pockets are eliminated. *Do not* use your hands or feet to compact the soil.

Step 6 Make a small berm two to four inches high in a ring around the buried roots. This directs water to the root zone when it rains and when you water. Fill the water ring, allowing the water to soak in slowly, and reshape the berm if it collapses.

Step 7 Fill the ring with water one last time and let it seep slowly into the soil. Then apply a layer of mulch two to three inches thick to cover the root zone and the berm. Don't let any mulch touch the trunk of a tree or the stems of a shrub.

Step 7

Transplanting the Right Way

Transplanting (digging up and moving a plant) is often necessary to keep a garden looking its best. As a garden evolves, growing conditions change. What was once a sunny spot near a young tree becomes a shady nook beneath a spreading canopy. The sun-loving plants that once performed well there gradually weaken and die. To avoid this, they must be dug up and moved to sunnier ground. Other plants may grow so fast they overstep their bounds, so their neighbors need to be shifted in order to make way for future growth. If a plant is in the wrong place, you can move it to a better spot where it will thrive.

Almost any plant can be transplanted, but some are easier than others. The smaller the better is a good rule to follow. New gardeners can confidently move herbaceous plants, but extra care should be taken with woodies. Newly planted trees and shrubs transplant easily because their roots have not fully established and spread, diminishing the potential for transplant shock. Still, even the largest tree can be relocated successfully if done right.

The best time to transplant is the same as the best time to plant. Do it in the spring. Herbaceous plants and small shrubs can be shifted in summer, but they must be watered consistently to survive, just like new plants. Large trees and shrubs should be dug when dormant, in late winter or earliest spring, before they bloom or leaf out. Conifers, like spruce and pine, can be transplanted in the fall, as can fleshy-rooted perennials like tree peonies.

Candidates for transplanting should be watered for several days before being dug to ensure the roots are fully hydrated and the root ball stays intact when lifted. If you are moving an actively growing plant, you should spray the foliage with an anti-dessicant to decrease water loss through transpiration and prevent wilting. (Such sprays are mainly used to protect trees and shrubs from cold-weather damage and are available at garden centers and online.) The shoots of established herbaceous perennials can be cut back to balance the roots with the shoots before or after transplanting.

Large woody plants should be root pruned in the fall to prepare for transplanting in the spring. With a nursery

Digging and moving plants is often necessary to keep a garden looking it's best.

spade, slice into the soil in a circle around the root zone at or beyond the circumference of the shoots or dig a small trench around the plant to expose the roots and prune them by hand. This condenses the root ball, making it easier to lift out of the ground. The roots respond to these cuts by producing tender feeding roots, increasing their ability to draw water and nutrients from the soil when replanted.

Prepare a planting hole for the transplant before you remove it from the ground. Take care to keep the root ball intact by placing it on a piece of burlap or in a spare pot before hoisting it into a wheelbarrow to move it. Follow the rest of the steps as if you were planting a container-grown plant.

How to Stake a Tree or Shrub

When you stake a tree or shrub, don't truss up the top of the tree. Stake the root ball into the ground, allowing the top of the tree to sway in the wind. Studies have shown that untethered trees form new roots faster. If the root ball doesn't tip or move, neither will the tree above.

To stake a root ball, you'll need one four-foot-long two-by-two wooden stake, a mallet, an old bicycle tire inner tube, a wood screw, a screwdriver or a cordless drill with a screwdriver bit, and a utility knife.

Step 1 Drive the wooden stake through the root ball and into the ground twelve to eighteen inches deep at a 45-degree angle near the trunk. Avoid damaging the roots by aiming the stake at a gap between root flares.

Step 2 Wrap a length of the rubber tube around the trunk just above the root flare and the stake in a figure-eight, placing it between them so they don't rub.

Step 3 Attach the rubber tube to the stake with a wood screw and trim off the excess tube. Inspect the stake throughout the year to ensure that it is not damaging the bark and is still functional.

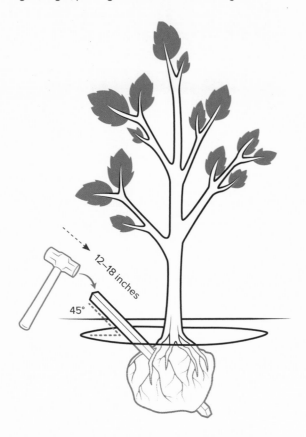

After-Planting Care

After you plant something comes the crucial period during which its roots are getting established in the soil, enabling the subsequent growth of healthy shoots. During this period, you must attend to the plant's need for water, pruning, and staking.

Watering The most important thing to help your new plants thrive, indeed survive, is ample water. Until it is fully established, the roots of a new plant don't reach very far out into the soil, which limits their supply of available moisture. It's up to the gardener to provide supplementary water for the first few months if rainfall isn't enough to ensure survival and growth. Soak the root ball as often as necessary so it never dries out.

Pruning New plants need to grow more roots, and shoots provide the resources and energy to make them, so keep the top of the plant intact. If, however, the shoots frequently wilt, prune some off until they balance with the roots. It's best to wait a year or two to do any corrective pruning on woody plants, but it's okay to remove flowers and damaged leaves on herbaceous plants. This directs energy to make more roots during their first season.

Staking Supporting a plant with stakes until its roots are fully formed should be done *only* if the plant needs it—for example, if it is planted on a steep slope or in a windy location. The weight of a balled-and-burlapped root ball will hold a tree steady under normal conditions, and smaller container plants won't tip if planted correctly. Bare-root plants, however, benefit from extra support until they break dormancy and the roots take hold.

Mulching Matters

More than a simple garden chore, mulching actually matters. Just like for anything else we do in the garden, we should always know why it's done, so here's the real story of why we mulch. Descriptions of the different types of mulch are then followed by advice on when and how to use them.

Why mulch?

Mulching is the final step when planting. Applying a two-to-three-inch layer of mulch around plants serves a number of important purposes.

Conserves soil moisture Mulch protects the soil from direct exposure to sun and wind, extending the time it takes for the root zone to dry out. Garden mulch mimics the natural conditions of the forest floor or meadow, where fallen leaves and dead plant parts blanket the ground, conserving moisture as they slowly decompose.

Regulates soil temperature A layer of mulch minimizes fluctuations in soil temperature between night and day, as well as the gradual changes occurring throughout the seasons. Plant roots can tolerate a wide range of temperatures, from below freezing in the winter to 100 degrees F or hotter in the summer, if the fluctuations occur over extended periods of time. Mulch keeps the soil temperature relatively stable, which plants prefer.

Adds nutrients and organic matter Organic mulches decompose over time. A layer of compost forms where the mulch material meets the soil and acts like a topdressing, introducing humus and improving soil structure, water-holding ability, and fertility. Fine-textured mulches break down quickly. Coarser materials take longer, but anything organic will biodegrade over time.

Limits weeds The thousands of dormant weed seeds in the soil need three things to germinate: water, the right temperature, and sunlight. A layer of mulch eliminates the light, making those seeds less likely to sprout. Mulch will not prevent weeds, but it can delay germination when applied *before* the weeds sprout on soil that is disturbed and exposed. It works only on weeds from seeds. Weeds that spread by underground roots will pop right through the mulch.

Prevents erosion and root or stem damage Bare ground is susceptible to erosion from wind and rain. The roots of living plants hold the soil in place, while foliage and mulch protect it from raindrops and runoff. A layer of mulch takes the place of cover plants and protects roots

Mulch and Nitrogen: Not to Worry

In the chapter on soil, you learned how carbon-rich organic matter biodegrades in conjunction with nitrogen during composting. Some gardeners fear that organic mulches like bark or pine straw will deplete nitrogen from the soil as they break down. This, however, occurs only on the surface, where the mulch touches the soil. There is still plenty of nitrogen down among the roots where plants absorb the nutrients they need. While organic mulch on the soil surface is fine, it should never be dug in where it would deplete the nitrogen around plant roots.

Shredded bark

Composition: Bark stripped from trees harvested for lumber—usually hemlock, oak, or cedar.

Texture and color: Coarse. Hemlock is medium-coarse and dark brown to black, oak is coarse and medium brown, cedar is medium-coarse and buff to brownish red.

Applications: Flat areas and large beds away from the house, and around trees.

Longevity: Variable. Hemlock lasts one year, oak lasts two years, and cedar lasts three or more years.

Sustainability: Marginal. By-product of the timber industry.

Availability and cost: Widely available. Cost determined by quality and regional sources.

Packaging: Bags and bulk.

otherwise exposed to damage from equipment, tools, or even a gardener's feet. Mulch rings around trees keep lawn mowers and string trimmers a safe distance from the trunk.

Provides a pleasing look A freshly mulched landscape bed is one of the most pleasing sights in the spring garden. When last year's layer of mulch has discolored or decomposed, the natural color of the new mulch complements the fresh green foliage and the flowers of trees, shrubs, and herbaceous plants.

Mulch materials

You can use a variety of materials, both organic and inorganic, as mulch. Factors to consider when you choose a material are the look, best applications, longevity, sustainability, availability, cost, and how the product is packaged.

Composted bark with peat moss

Composition: Shredded bark composted with peat moss.

Texture and color: Fine. Dark brown.

Applications: Landscape beds close to the house, slopes, and as topdressing to improve soil.

Longevity: Single season.

Sustainability: Minimal. Bark and peat moss must be harvested.

Availability and cost: Limited availability. Twenty to 30 percent more expensive than ordinary shredded bark.

Packaging: Bags and bulk.

Pine nuggets

Composition: Chunks of pine bark from harvested trees.

Texture and color: Fine (a half inch) to very coarse (six inches). Light to dark brown.

Applications: Useful throughout the garden due to diversity of texture and decorative nature. Not effective on slopes or where water collects, because they float.

Longevity: Two to ten years, depending on texture size.

Sustainability: Marginal. By-product of the timber industry.

Availability and cost: Widely available. Price increases with nugget size.

Packaging: Bags only.

Pine straw

Composition: Pine needles from longleaf and loblolly pine trees.

Texture and color: Fine. Red when new, bleaching to silver-gray in full sun.

Applications: Large areas, steep slopes, and around acid-loving plants. Lightweight and easy to spread.

Longevity: Single season in the shade, needs replacing twice yearly in full sun.

Sustainability: Exceptional. Naturally occurring and raked from the forest floor.

Availability and cost: Regionally available. Cost determined by proximity to longleaf and loblolly pine groves.

Packaging: Bales and bags.

Straw

Composition: Stalks from harvested wheat (usually), not to be confused with hay, which serves as animal feed and often contains seeds that will sprout if used as mulch.

Texture and color: Coarse. Buff.

Applications: Purely functional settings, like vegetable plots or as erosion control on slopes. Lightweight, easy to spread and rake out. Susceptible to wind upon initial application but knits together when watered.

Longevity: Partial season.

Sustainability: Very good. By-product of another use.

Availability and cost: Easy to find and affordable.

Packaging: Bales and bags.

Stone

Composition: Quarried stone chips and harvested river pebbles.

Texture and color: Very fine to very coarse. Brown, red, blue, black, green, and buff.

Applications: Decorative beds with specimen plantings. Desert and semi-arid climates.

Longevity: Decades.

Sustainability: Good, due to longevity.

Availability and cost: Widely available. Cost depends on regional geology.

Packaging: Bags and bulk.

Leaves

Composition: Shredded fallen leaves from deciduous trees.

Texture and color: Coarse. Yellow, red, orange, and brown. Color fades rapidly.

Applications: Useful on established plantings to suppress weeds early in the season and maintain soil quality, and on new beds to improve poor soil.

Longevity: Single season or replace twice a year.

Sustainability: Exceptional.

Availability and cost: Widely available and free. Run a lawnmower over a pile of leaves in your yard to shred.

Packaging: Roadside piles and bags.

Wood chips and twigs

Composition: Branches too small or not suitable for firewood fed into a wood chipper.

Texture and color: Very coarse. Buff to brown.

Applications: Purely functional settings, like vacant plots or new tree plantings far from the house. On a rustic path.

Longevity: Several seasons.

Sustainability: Very good. By-product of other work.

Availability and cost: Readily available from arborists and often free.

Packaging: Bulk only.

Grass clippings

Composition: Mowed lawn grass.

Texture and color: Fine. Rich green quickly fades to yellow, then brown.

Applications: Can be used sparingly in established gardens, mixed with leaves, combining browns and greens to make a rich compost. Keep off edible gardens due to residue of chemicals commonly used on turfgrass.

Longevity: Single season.

Sustainability: Very good. By-product of other work.

Availability and cost: Readily available and free wherever lawns exist.

Packaging: None.

Compost

Composition: Organic matter, humus.

Texture and color: Fine. Dark brown to black.

Applications: You and your garden have reached the pinnacle of perfection when the only mulch you apply is compost. It means your ornamental plantings are fully mature and knit together, exposing no bare ground during the growing season, and your edible garden is equally bountiful.

Longevity: Single season or apply bimonthly during growing season.

Sustainability: Exceptional. The ultimate mulch.

Availability and cost: Readily available from local and regional sources. Homemade is free, store-bought price depends on the quality.

Packaging: Bulk and bags.

Mulches to Avoid

Ever innovative, landscapers have developed mulches from unconventional materials. Dyed bark puts a colorful spin on the decorative attributes of mulch, while shredded rubber provides longevity and a use for old tires. Both do everything normal mulches do, but with one consequential disqualifying trait. Residual chemicals in the dyes of colored mulch and from the vulcanization process of the rubber introduce dangerous contaminants into the soil. This makes their use anathema to any responsible gardener. Show that you know better and don't use them.

Boycott cypress mulches, commonly derived from entire bald cypress trees harvested from the wild. Trees are cut down faster than they can regrow, upsetting the balance of the wetland ecosystems in which they live.

Never use peat moss as a mulch, because it repels water. Although shredded paper can function as a mulch, it won't last long, and glossy magazines and catalogs—anything with colored inks—shouldn't be used. You might try recycled glass, but only if it has been processed so it's smooth.

Spread mulch by hand close to plants and avoid touching trunks and stems.

To figure out how much mulch you'll need to cover an area three inches deep, multiply the length and width of the area in feet by .25 (a quarter of a foot, or three inches). The result will be the quantity in cubic feet, which is how bagged mulch is sold. There are twenty-seven cubic feet in a cubic yard, which is how bulk mulch is sold.

How and when to mulch

Mulching is simple. Spread two to three inches of your preferred material over any bare ground. Less will work, but be sure no soil is showing. More than three inches is too much and can inhibit water and oxygen infiltration to plant roots. Dump the mulch in piles around the bed and spread it with a rake in open areas and by hand close to plants. Don't let the mulch touch stems or trunks on woody plants or smother small herbaceous shoots. Mulch after planting to help get new plants off to a healthy start. Conservation of soil moisture is of utmost importance, as is regulation of soil temperature while plant roots establish themselves.

Mulch volcanoes can harm trees and should be avoided.

Mulch mistakes

Mulch volcanoes are problematic and should be avoided. Piling up biodegradable material around the trunk of a tree invites insects and disease. This can compromise the protective layer of bark, resulting in stunted growth or rot with irreversible damage, even death.

Piling mulch too high around a woody plant can also cause girdling roots to develop, just as planting trees too deep can. Meristematic tissue in a stem that is buried will develop into roots. As they grow into the loose mulch, these roots wrap around the tree and can, in time, girdle the vascular phloem beneath the bark.

Proper planting and mulching mark the beginning of a plant's life in your garden. While the importance of getting plants off to a good start should never be minimized, the responsibility of a gardener extends well beyond these first steps. Once the plants are in place, continued care must follow. Watering and feeding are essential tasks and are the focus of the next chapter.

Spring applications of mulch are common, but there is no need to mulch throughout the garden every season. Apply mulch selectively on bare spots and where it is less than an inch thick. If the depth is adequate but the mulch looks tired, fluff it with a rake or hoe and sprinkle a light layer of fresh material on top to make it look new again.

A fall mulch freshening is useful in both warm and cold climates. In warm climates, where the mulch continues to biodegrade year-round, a fresh layer in the fall provides a nice look through the winter months when plantings are less lush. Gardens in regions with frigid winters benefit from additional late-season mulch to protect plant roots from extreme variations in soil temperature.

watering and feeding

Balancing Between Nature and Nurture

"Where Theory and Practice Meet" is the slogan of the School of Professional Horticulture at the New York Botanical Garden. Posted above the entrance to the hall where thousands of students have attended classes over the decades, this slogan epitomizes the best way to learn gardening. Like these students, you too have learned lessons about plants and soil that can be applied directly to daily gardening assignments. Watering and feeding are two such tasks that put knowledge into practice. They account for significant time spent in the garden, and when done right, each activity contributes to achieving the ultimate aim of growing healthy, happy plants.

The previous chapter taught you how to get plants into the ground. Now let's explore how to make these plants thrive. During your early days of gardening it's often enough if the plants just stay alive, but as mere survival becomes commonplace you'll want more from what you grow. Plantings flourish when you strike a balance between what nature provides and the assistance only a gardener can supply. Learn the right way to water and fertilize, and your plants will prosper, feeding a desire for more beauty and greater bounty.

Water in the Garden

Watering requirements and recommendations are a common conundrum for gardeners of all experience levels. Part of the problem is the variability of water provided to a garden by nature. While seasonal precipitation typically follows reliable trends, daily or weekly rain is never guaranteed, an uncertainty that can stress plants and gardeners alike.

Droughts and the water restrictions they produce pose significant problems for those who rely on supplemental water in their gardens. Rather than fret or pray for rain, avoid the slow demise of established landscape plants or the loss of your edibles crop by planning for dry times. Assume control by improving the soil's field capacity and selecting plants suited to the rainfall trends in your region. Even then, what nature provides must sometimes be supplemented. Do it smartly, with an understanding of plants' needs.

Why plants need water

"Water is the driver of Nature," wrote Leonardo da Vinci. Gardener or not, he certainly knew what he was talking about. There is no life without water, for us and for plants. This is how water is used by plants during times of growth:

Cell expansion Plant cells will not divide or elongate without water. No water = no growth.

Conduction of nutrients Without water, the flow of minerals through the vascular system of the plant stops.

Gardener's Glossary

Transpiration is the process whereby plants absorb water through the roots and give off water vapor through pores in their leaves.

A **watering rose** is the showerhead at the end of a hose or watering can spout that breaks the water into a soft stream.

A **soaker hose** is a garden hose made of permeable rubber that slowly leaks water along its length when under pressure.

Waterwise gardening means growing plants with the least amount of supplemental irrigation.

Drought tolerance is a plant's ability to endure regular or frequent dry spells with few or no detrimental effects.

Turgidity Water inside a plant exerts pressure on cell walls so herbaceous stems stand straight and leaves open fully.

Propagation A seed will not germinate and meristematic tissue will not respond without water.

Photosynthesis Photosynthesis cannot occur without water.

Transpiration Plants cannot perspire and cool themselves without water.

Transpiration rates and water needs

Most of the water plants absorb from the soil is ultimately released through transpiration. A fifty-foot shade tree loses up to sixty gallons of water per hour, and a healthy tomato plant will absorb and release at least thirty gallons of water throughout a growing season. The rate of transpiration, though determined by environmental factors, is directly related to plant selection, soil improvement, and watering practices, all of which gardeners can actively influence.

How to Conserve Water in the Garden

No matter where you garden, water is a resource that should never be taken for granted. Proper soil management, smart plant selection, and intelligent irrigation techniques work together to conserve the water we use to grow our gardens. Rain barrels and cisterns, for example, are great ways to collect and store water for future use.

To make use of every drop of water that reaches your garden, from spigot or sky, you must increase the ground's water-holding capacity by adding humus to the soil. As you learned earlier, soil high in organic content holds water like a sponge, making it available to plants as they need it. As the foundation for your landscaping, grow a combination of plants that includes species that use less water. If water restrictions arise, these plants must fend for themselves while limited resources are directed to seasonal crops that require regular watering.

Watering established trees and shrubs should be reserved for times of extended drought. Mature specimens that have been in the ground five or more years should have extensive root systems capable of absorbing all the water they need if the soil has been properly managed and the plants are the right match for the region. If an extended drought threatens established woodies, help them survive by soaking their root zone twice a month until the rains return. Focus limited water resources on the most vulnerable and valuable plants and use mulches to slow water loss due to evaporation.

Day-to-day atmospheric conditions affect transpiration rates and thus the amount of water being absorbed from the soil by plants. Increased sunlight, temperature, and wind along with low humidity increase transpiration, while decreased sunlight, temperature, and wind along with high humidity decrease transpiration. So overall weather conditions, not just rainfall, determine when and how much water must be given to the garden. Transpiration rates change over the course of a year, a month, a week, or a day, sometimes even by the hour. That's why smart gardeners step outside or check the weather forecast before deciding whether to water.

Determining whether it's a good day to water isn't as simple as asking if it's sunny or hot. For example, if the weather is hot and humid with no wind and lots of clouds, three of those factors contribute to a low transpiration rate, so established plants probably don't need to be watered. What if the next day is hot, humid, sunny, and windy? Now three of those factors contribute to an increase in transpiration, so it might be a good day to water the garden. Gardeners must evaluate the conditions each day and act accordingly.

Plants' needs for water vary, so don't fall for any tip that tells you plants need a certain amount of water per week. It's an oversimplification that leads many new gardeners astray. Focus instead on soil improvement and fostering adaptable plants.

high transpiration   **low transpiration**

full sunlight

low sunlight

low humidity

high humidity

100°
90°
80°
70°
60°
50°
40°
30°

100°
90°
80°
70°
60°
50°
40°
30°

high temperature

high winds

no wind

low temperature

Atmospheric conditions affect rates of transpiration.

Wet soil (left) increases transpiration and dry soil (right) decreases it.

How to Interpret Plants' Water Preferences

You'll find a plant's water preference stated on the tag it bears at the nursery, and you can also look it up online, in plant catalogs, and in reference books. Ideally, when you choose plants for different areas of your garden, you match their water preferences to existing conditions. Here's what the various moisture preference categories mean:

Continuously wet The soil is always soaked. These are conditions for water lovers like weeping willow and wild cardinal flower. Soil like this is common in riparian zones along rivers and ponds, in natural wetlands, and in low spots and depressions.

Moderately moist The soil never completely dries out. The vast majority of landscape and edible plants thrive in this sort of soil. This condition is typical of garden loam with good field capacity and proper drainage.

Dry between watering The soil dries out completely before more water is added. Succulents want dry soil or else their roots rot, and heat lovers like geraniums, petunias, and bougainvillea do best when allowed to dry out. A terracotta pot with a topdressing of pebbles set in the sun is the best way to duplicate these conditions.

While all plants have distinct water preferences, some plants are considered drought tolerant because they are not damaged by drought. Drought-tolerant plants do not necessarily *prefer* dry conditions; they *tolerate* dry conditions. For example, a pine and a willow will thrive equally with ample water, but during a drought the pine will endure while the willow may be stunted or die. Many drought-tolerant plants—such as lavender, sage, and agave—also prefer dry conditions in general.

Aside from atmospheric conditions, soil moisture availability, a.k.a. field capacity, affects plant transpiration. If the soil has a low field capacity and dries out quickly, plants will respond by slowing their metabolism to decrease their water needs. If this happens too often the plant will be stunted, and parts may even die to compensate for low levels of available moisture.

Before you water, check the soil around the root zone of the plants by pushing your index finger about three inches into the soil. If the soil feels dry, go ahead and water. If it feels damp, don't. Plants suffer as much from overwatering as from underwatering. You can also tell that a plant needs water if it's wilting, though some plants—like hydrangea and ligularia—commonly droop in midday heat and recover by evening.

Leaf size and construction also determine how much water a plant uses and loses. The surface area of a leaf is directly proportional to the rate of transpiration. Big leaves have lots of pores, so they transpire more. Tiny leaves have fewer pores, so they lose water more slowly. This includes needle-shaped foliage, like that of conifers. Many plants have evolved ways to slow transpiration and to make the most of soil moisture. Some have leaves covered with wax or oils that seal the pores and limit water loss. Some have fuzzy leaves that decrease wind exposure and slow evaporation. Succulents have fleshy leaves that retain water to get them through dry times.

A leaf's size, structure, and surface also affect transpiration, with large leaves transpiring more than small leaves, and waxy or fuzzy leaves transpiring less.

When and how much to water

There's a right way to water and there's a wrong way to water. Water your garden right and your plants will thrive.

Early in the morning Make sure your plants have the water they need when they need it. Water at the beginning of the day so metabolism won't be disrupted by lack of water. Athletes hydrate before working out, and the same goes for plants. However, if you can't water in the morning it's okay to water thirsty plants in the evening or anytime you notice a need.

Long and deep, not short and sweet A common mistake among gardeners is to tease rather than appease a plant's need for water. It's best for the plant if you soak the soil so it is fully charged with water to maximum field capacity. Wetting the surface doesn't get it done, and shallow watering encourages plant roots to concentrate in the top few inches of soil, limiting their absorptive surface area while making them root-bound. Deep watering stimulates deep root growth. When watering, recreate an all-day soaking rain, not a passing shower. Remember that less frequent deep watering based on soil conditions, transpiration rate, and growing season is more effective than frequent shallow watering.

Water the soil, *not* the plants Technically, we don't water plants, we water the soil the plants live in. This is especially true for established gardens, where the roots of plants grow throughout the beds. Roots can't grow where there's no water. By watering the entire bed and not just the root zone of individual plants, we encourage roots to spread. This helps plants survive occasional dry spells because their root system will have expanded far and wide ... and deep.

Watering methods

While rainwater is often sufficient for established gardens in climates where it rains regularly throughout the summer, relying solely on rainwater isn't recommended for edible gardens or when starting new plants. Since relying on rain works only when growing adaptable plants in soil with good field capacity, new gardens also need supplemental water until the ground is improved.

How to Water New Plants

Weeks 1 and 2 Soak the root ball daily.

Week 3 Soak the root ball and adjacent area between plants every other day.

Week 4 Soak the root ball and adjacent area between plants two to three times during the week.

Week 5 and beyond Soak the root ball once each week and water the adjacent area between plants one or two times per week for the rest of the growing season. In times of drought, add an extra watering each week.

A hose with a watering wand makes hand watering easy.

Hand watering is the preferred way to water a garden. Hand watering by can or hose allows you to water plants selectively, giving those that need it what they want and those that don't need it nothing at all. It also gets the gardener out in the garden where small issues can be spotted before they become big problems. I use daily or weekly watering visits to check and inspect my plants. By combining a few strategically placed hoses that have watering wands and a couple of watering cans, you can water any garden by hand.

The best watering can is well built and made of metal or durable plastic. Different sizes and shapes are useful for different applications, but a one- or two-gallon can with a long spout, a removable rose, and handles on the top and the side for easy carrying and pouring is perfectly versatile.

Lightweight or medium-grade hoses are easier to wrangle than heavy ones. I prefer black hoses over green hoses because black recedes into the shadows when hoses are left in place. Stash them under bushes and behind walls wherever there's a spigot. Watering with a hose requires a wand: a three-foot aluminum pipe with an on/off valve at the end that couples with the hose and a water breaker, or rose, at the other end. The rose allows the water to hit the soil with a soft splash while providing enough volume to rival a steady stream. Use the wand to deliver water directly to the soil by sticking the rose beneath the foliage down around the root zone.

Leaky, broken, or punctured hoses can easily be fixed with a good repair kit consisting of connectors and rubber washers. Also consider quick-release connectors. These fixtures make connecting hoses to spigots and to other hoses a snap, eliminating the need to laboriously twist them on and off. Buy brass instead of plastic for a lifetime of leak-free use.

Irrigation is a viable option even though hand watering is best, but be aware of its costs and limitations. The price of professional installation for top-quality systems is formidable, and upkeep expenses for large systems are onerous. Worse yet, their inability to apply water intelligently when and where it is needed make most irrigation systems inefficient and wasteful. Intelligent, conservative irrigation can play a role in watering a garden, but you need to know a few things about the different types and their best use before investing in a system.

Water inside a black hose sitting in the sun gets hot, so always run the water until it comes out cold before spraying the garden.

For a perfect emerald green lawn all summer long, regardless of drought or expense, install rotor head irrigation. These heads throw a lot of water a long way and are the most effective means of watering large areas of low-growing plants.

Useful for small patches of lawn, spray heads can be adjusted to spray a cone of water from 5 to 360 degrees, and elevated four inches to four feet or more. Keep them out of garden beds, where they hurt plants with their direct spray, promote fungus issues by continually soaking the foliage, and stain adjacent walks and walls.

How to Water a Lawn

The best way to water a lawn is just like for every other part of the garden, with long, deep soakings. This encourages turfgrass roots to grow deep into the soil, helping the lawn survive dry spells. Traditional lawns must be watered several times a week to stay lush and green, but you can grow a sustainable lawn that needs much less water by using alternative grass species, promoting an organic soil, and allowing the lawn to go dormant during droughts.

Several types of portable sprinklers—such as oscillating, pulsating, whirling, and stationary rings—can be hooked up to a hose and positioned right where they're needed. These handy devices are perfect as temporary irrigation for lawn renovations or starting plants from seed. However, they should not be relied on long-term due to their inefficient use of water.

Drip is the only irrigation method I recommend for garden beds because it delivers water directly to the soil. Drip hoses with built-in emitters are laid on the ground and covered with mulch. Emitters can be arranged throughout a bed in a grid or other pattern to water not just individual plants but the soil between plants as well. Individual emitters for container plants can be tailored to match the size of the pot and the water needs of the plant.

Made of permeable rubber, soaker hoses leak water slowly onto the soil. Use them for new plantings and remove them once plants are established. They are perfect for edible gardens, where daily overhead watering can harm leafy crops, and are easily removed to prepare the ground for planting or during harvest.

Timers make any type of irrigation—whether a fully automated system, several soaker hoses, or a lone oscillating sprinkler—more convenient. Professionally installed systems come with a programmable control panel that turns individual watering stations on and off as needed. Temporary installations can be controlled with manual or digital timers hooked up between the spigot and the hose. The ability to adjust the duration and frequency of watering is the key to a good irrigation system.

A three-year irrigation plan to establish new plants

This method is the best way to ensure the survival of new plantings. It transitions plants over the course of three years from newly planted to well established, focusing on the development of extensive root systems that will carry the plants forward into maturity. Start with the recommended watering times but adjust these times up or down as you assess the actual water-holding capacity of your soil and the needs of your plants. Add time if the ground dries out quickly, subtract time if it stays soggy.

Year 1: Help new plants survive their first season After new plantings are installed, lay soaker hoses in a sinuous grid pattern throughout the entire planting bed. For large trees, make several loops around their root zone to ensure they receive extra water. Hook the soaker hose up to a regular hose and run it to the closest water spigot. Between the hose and the spigot, install a digital timer to automate the flow of water on and off. Set the timer to water every day for an hour or more depending on sun exposure and plant type. As spring turns to summer, increase the time the water runs but decrease the frequency to two or three times a week. When summer turns to fall, decrease the frequency to once or twice a week as daytime temperatures drop. When the season ends and the plants go dormant, remove the garden hose and the timer and store them for the winter. Leave the soaker hoses in place.

Year 2: Aid plant establishment during their second season Toward the end of a winter rainy season, reattach the timer to the spigot and the garden hose to the timer and the soaker hoses. When temperatures are consistently 70 degrees F or warmer, set the timer to run for two hours twice a week. If it doesn't rain for two weeks, double the time the water runs until it rains again. As summer turns to fall and temperatures cool, decrease watering to two hours once a week. When the season ends and the plants go dormant, remove the garden hose and the timer and store them for the winter. Leave the soaker hoses in place.

Year 3: Keep plants happy through the summer heat In early summer, reattach the timer to the spigot and the garden hose to the timer and the soaker hoses. Do not turn the water on until temperatures are consistently 80 degrees F or warmer. Set the timer to run one hour once a week. If it doesn't rain for two weeks, manually run the water for three hours once a week until it rains again. As summer turns to fall and temperatures cool, shut the water off. If there is a late season drought, manually run the water for three hours to charge the soil with moisture. When the plants go dormant, remove the timer, garden hose, and soaker hoses and store them all for reuse on another planting.

This entire sequence and schedule can also be performed with permanently installed drip irrigation. After the third year the drip hoses stay in place and the system becomes an insurance policy against drought, turned on and off manually as conditions warrant or to support moisture-loving plants in gardens with hot, dry summers. Use irrigation as a supplement, not a primary source of water for your plants. Plants addicted to irrigation are less adaptable to seasonal stresses. Raised with a little tough love, they will survive periodic adversity.

How to Water Plants in Pots

Not all gardeners garden in the ground. Apartment dwellers must grow plants exclusively in pots or planters, and many homeowners with land also grow plants in containers on porches or patios. Plants grown outdoors in pots need special care because they dry out more quickly than plants in the open ground, and the limited root zone in small pots dries out even more quickly than in large pots.

Check your containers daily. If the top two inches of soil are dry, give the pot a good deep watering. If the soil is damp, do not water. Containers must have holes in the bottom to allow drainage. If they don't, the plants will get waterlogged when it rains. Pots placed on decks or terraces should have pot feet, flat supports made of plastic, clay, or cement, placed underneath to allow for airflow and prevent stains to the surface they sit on. I don't use saucers under my outdoor containers because I want the water to drain freely from the pot. Saucers are for indoor pots to protect furniture and floors.

Slowly apply water from a watering can or wand to the potting mix beneath the leaves of the plants until you see water coming out the bottom of the pot. This means the potting mix is at full field capacity. If water immediately runs out the bottom, the plant may be root-bound and need replanting. Persnickety gardeners top-dress container plants with gravel above a layer of sand on top of the potting mix. This allows the water to slowly seep in and keeps the potting mix from splashing out.

Water container plants from the top, and use saucers for indoor plants.

Fertilizer Facts

Some say the best fertilizer is a gardener's footsteps. I used that line for years in my classes until an insightful student pointed out that too many footsteps compact the soil. "Ha-ha!" I replied. "Now you're figuring it out." So, what *is* the best fertilizer? That answer depends as much on you, the gardener, as it does on the plants you grow. Once you know a few facts about fertilizer, you can decide for yourself.

Fact 1 There is a difference between compost and fertilizer. Adding compost to your soil improves its fertility by increasing cation exchange. Adding fertilizer to your soil adds nutrients that can then be absorbed by plants through cation exchange.

Fact 2 There are six nutrients plants must have in large amounts. Three of them—oxygen (O), hydrogen (H), and carbon (C)—come from air and water. The other three—nitrogen (N), phosphorus (P), and potassium (K), called macronutrients—are sourced from the soil.

Fact 3 There are three essential nutrients plants use in moderate amounts—calcium (Ca), sulfur (S), and magnesium (Mg), often referred to collectively as secondary nutrients. These too are sourced from the soil.

Fact 4 There are seven mineral nutrients plants need in trace amounts—boron (B), chlorine (Cl), copper (Cu), iron (Fe), manganese (Mn), molybdenum (Mo), and zinc (Zn), dubbed micronutrients. They also come from the soil.

Nitrogen, phosphorus, and potassium (N-P-K) are the primary plant nutrients found in fertilizers. The three numbers prominently displayed on all fertilizer bags correspond to the percentage, by weight, of these nutrients in the blend. For example, a forty-pound bag of fertilizer labeled "10-10-10" contains four pounds each of nitrogen, phosphorus, and potassium. Each nutrient is essential for the growth of certain plant parts. Nitrogen makes leaves; phosphorus makes flowers, fruits, and roots; and

Macronutrients nitrogen, phosphorus, and potassium are the primary plant nutrients found in fertilizers, indicated by the three prominently displayed numbers.

potassium is required for overall plant health. Sometimes this is simplified to say: "N makes leaves, P makes flowers, and K makes roots."

Sulfur, calcium, and magnesium (S-Ca-Mg) as secondary nutrients are occasionally specified in fertilizer blends but are more often sold separately as supplementary amendments. Sulfur helps plants form necessary enzymes and proteins. It also aids plants with disease resistance and seed formation. Calcium is crucial for holding together cell walls, and magnesium is a building block of chlorophyll. Deficiencies in any of these nutrients limit plant growth.

Micronutrients (B-Cl-Cu-Fe-Mn-Mo-Zn), though needed only in trace amounts, are essential for the complete health and metabolism of all plants. Iron (Fe) deficiencies, for example, are quite common, signaled by the yellowing of leaves. Lack of other micronutrients is more difficult to discern, but since only small amounts are needed, most organic fertilizers provide ample amounts.

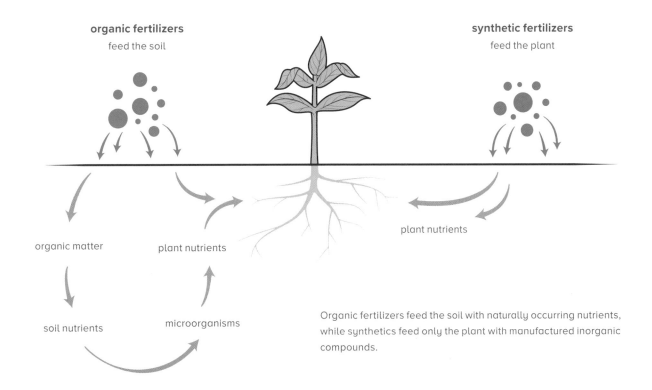

Organic fertilizers feed the soil with naturally occurring nutrients, while synthetics feed only the plant with manufactured inorganic compounds.

Gardener's Glossary

Organic gardening is growing plants in a living soil without the use of synthetic fertilizers, pesticides, or herbicides.

N-P-K is the shorthand used to indicate the three macronutrients of nitrogen, phosphorus, and potassium, respectively, using their symbols from the periodic table of elements.

A **micronutrient** is a mineral necessary in trace amounts for plant health and growth.

Organics versus synthetics

Fertilizers can be divided into two classes: organic and synthetic. Organic fertilizers deliver nutrients in the form of naturally occurring mineral, plant, and animal ingredients, such as blood meal and bat guano for nitrogen, rock phosphate and bone meal for phosphorus, and kelp meal and greensand for potassium. Synthetic fertilizers deliver these same nutrients as manufactured inorganic compounds: ammonium nitrate for nitrogen, ammonium phosphate for phosphorus, and potassium nitrate for potassium. Either form can be added where plant roots will absorb them directly, but the very best fertilizer for all garden ground comes from naturally organic sources.

The problem with most synthetic fertilizers is that they contain only N, P, and K. This leads to deficiencies in secondary nutrients and micronutrients that must be supplemented with additional fertilizers. Organic fertilizers avoid this issue because their natural composition provides more than enough of all necessary trace elements, and in most cases, adequate amounts of the secondary nutrients.

Synthetic fertilizers are by nature stronger than organics because they are manufactured to be so. This means it takes a smaller amount of synthetic fertilizer to get the necessary N, P, and K into the soil than it takes when using organic fertilizer. While this might sound like an argument for synthetics, actually it's not. The overwhelming strength of synthetics makes them dangerous. It's easy to damage plants with synthetic fertilizers that contain high amounts of nitrogen and phosphorus, but it's nearly impossible to overdo it with an organic fertilizer. The tender roots and shoots of transplants and seedlings are especially susceptible to burning from concentrated synthetic fertilizers.

The most compelling argument against synthetic fertilizers is that they have one nasty side effect: they kill the soil. The salt compounds used to bind N, P, and K into inorganic forms harm the microbiota living in the soil. As a result, synthetics actually negate the positive effects of adding compost because they literally kill these living ingredients.

When choosing between synthetic and organic fertilizers, consider this analogy. Growing organically is like having a balanced diet, one in which you get your daily nutrients from the food you eat. Growing with synthetics is like living on vitamin supplements alone. Which is better? One might argue, "If vitamins can help balance a human's diet, why can't synthetic fertilizers supplement what plants need?" The answer is simple. All fertilizers act like vitamins for plants, but a living soil provides a balanced diet. Synthetics are unnecessary because all the mineral nutrients plants need can be found in organic form, which will not harm the living nature of the soil. Both forms work, but it's up to you to choose the type of garden you will grow and the kind of gardener you will be: always organic or sometimes synthetic.

Fertilizer delivery methods

The key to understanding fertilizer is to get that feeding the soil feeds the plants. How we deliver the nutrients to the soil is the question. Fertilizers come in several forms. The best choice depends on the situation, whether for a

When to Use Synthetics

The only place I might use synthetic fertilizer is in a flowerpot of annuals. The goal of growing annuals is to make lots of flowers throughout the season, which powerful synthetics can accomplish. The plants and the potting mix go into the compost pile at season's end, where their inorganic properties are neutralized.

Never use a synthetic fertilizer in a pot with a long-lived plant, like a small tree or shrub, or with edibles. Promote a living soil and stay organic instead.

Synthetic fertilizer can give annuals the boost they need to make lots of flowers throughout the growing season.

flower bed, a lawn, or plants in pots. Whatever the form, the ultimate goal is to get N, P, and K—as well as all other nutrients the plants need—into the soil around their roots.

▲ **Granular** fertilizer is the most common form of fertilizer. Easily spread by hand or machine, granular fertilizers are sold in bags that range from five to fifty pounds. Synthetics come in colorful pellets while organics are more like bits of grit and dust. Granular fertilizers are perfect for site-specific feeding around the root zones of new plants and broadcasting across large expanses of lawn or other ground cover.

◀ **Emulsions** of fish and seaweed are concentrated organic fertilizers from the sea that are mixed with water to apply. They include a balance of the mineral nutrients plants need, especially trace elements. The main benefit of emulsions is that they are a way to apply organic fertilizer as a liquid, which is useful for container plants. Sold in quart, liter, or gallon jugs, these malodorous concoctions can be mixed at varied concentrations listed on the label to safely deliver a mild or strong dose.

▶ **Soluble** fertilizers are synthetic N, P, and K bound in salt compounds that dissolve in water. They are super concentrated, with N-P-K percentage numbers typically in the double digits. This means the solution must be properly diluted or plants will be burned by too much nitrogen or phosphorus. To be safe, always cut the recommended application rate in half.

◀ **Compost** isn't fertilizer, it's a fertility enhancer. Compost does, however, contain many of the mineral nutrients plants need, especially secondary and trace elements, another reason why adding compost to your garden beds is the best way to feed your plants. One limitation of compost is that top-dressing small potted plants and large areas like lawns is impractical. The solution is compost tea—tea made from compost. Make it at home by putting a shovelful of compost inside a cheesecloth sack and soaking it in a large bucket of water set in the sun. In a few days you have compost tea. There are also machines that make large amounts quickly. I prefer the most basic technique: add a few scoops of compost to a bucket of water and start stirring.

Other amendments

You can apply any number of other amendments besides packaged fertilizer to help plants get the nutrients they need as well as improve the soil. This is when gardening gets fun and individualized. For example, I put blood meal around my lettuce. It adds nitrogen for leaf production, and the smell frightens rabbits that might nibble on the new shoots. Most experienced gardeners, like good cooks in the kitchen, have similar tricks of their own, often based on purely anecdotal evidence. There is a tinge of folklore to this aspect of gardening, so my advice is to learn the qualities of these amendments and base your use of them on what you have learned about how plants and soil work.

Greensand is a soil conditioner mined from the ocean floor. It improves soil structure and increases field capacity while providing potassium, iron, and magnesium.

Garden gypsum is a naturally occurring mineral that opens compacted clay soil and is high in the secondary nutrient calcium. It helps reduce salt levels in coastal soils but should not be added to soils already high in calcium.

Aluminum sulfate is a chemical compound that adds sulfur to increase acidity. Use it to balance highly alkaline soils or around acid-loving plants like conifers, hollies, azaleas, and blueberries.

Vermiculite is a type of mineral made from aluminum, iron, and magnesium silicates. Neutral in pH, it increases water retention and fertility while aerating the soil. It can pose a health hazard if the dust is inhaled, so handle it wisely.

▲ **Slow-release** fertilizers do exactly what the name claims: they release N, P, and K into the soil slowly over time. This is most advantageous when added to pots of annual flowers for a boost in bloom production throughout the summer. The most common variety are BB-size balls filled with synthetic, soluble N-P-K. Small holes in the balls allow the fertilizer inside to gradually release when it rains or when the pot is watered. It's a nifty trick, but it's still a synthetic. Organic versions of slow-release fertilizers are gypsum and rice hulls, which break down over many months.

TOP ROW, FROM LEFT TO RIGHT: greensand, garden gypsum, aluminum sulfate. MIDDLE ROW, FROM LEFT TO RIGHT: vermiculite, garden lime, blood meal. BOTTOM ROW, FROM LEFT TO RIGHT: bone meal, worm castings, leaf mold

Garden lime is mined from mineral deposits of ancient limestone. Powdered or pelletized, its main use is to increase the pH of acid soils. It also promotes beneficial bacteria that enhance the living nature of the soil.

Blood meal, or dried blood, typically comes from cows but can be from any animal. An excellent source of nitrogen, it boosts leaf production while slightly increasing soil acidity.

Bone meal is ground-up animal bones. An excellent source of phosphorus, it can be added to flower and vegetable beds to boost blooms and increase fruit production.

Worm castings consist of the digested soil that has passed through a worm. Containing every nutrient required for plant growth, castings are ready to use straight from the worm without composting.

Leaf mold is nothing more than leaves that have decomposed over time. Added as organic matter to garden soils, leaf mold improves aggregation, field capacity, and cation exchange.

How to Read a Fertilizer Label

The front of the bag is marketing. What you need to know about a fertilizer is found on the back of the bag.

N-P-K numbers Written prominently in a large font, this sequence of three numbers indicates the percentage, by weight, of these nutrients in the blend. A large first number means there is high nitrogen content, meaning the fertilizer is good for making leaves and therefore useful for a lawn, ferns, or edible greens. A large second number means there is ample phosphorus in the bag, making this a bloom-boosting formula useful for growing flowers and fruiting plants. A high third number means there is plenty of potassium to promote strong roots. Single-digit, nonuniform numbers (for example, 3-5-4) usually mean it's organic. Double-digit or uniform numbers (for example, 20-20-20) mean it's synthetic.

Intended use This line tells you which plants the fertilizer is intended for, though a savvy gardener can deduce this from the N-P-K numbers. An "All Purpose Fertilizer" is a good bet if you want to use it on everything, but targeted fertilizers are useful if you have specific plants that you want to feed, like tomatoes or roses.

Guaranteed analysis This part of the label shows the percentage of available nitrogen, phosphorus, potassium, and other minerals in the bag's contents. The first three percentages are the same as the N-P-K numbers.

Ingredients This lists the ingredients the mineral nutrients are derived from. On a bag of organic fertilizer, the ingredients list will sound like a selection of grains and minerals, such as bone meal, corn gluten meal, and rock phosphate. On a bag of synthetic fertilizer, it will read like a chemical prescription: ammonium nitrate, ammonium phosphate, potassium nitrate.

Additional biota Soil food web ingredients such as mycorrhizal fungi and beneficial bacillus are often added to organic fertilizers to promote a living soil that helps plants absorb the nutrients included in the blend. These ingredients have a life span, so if they are included check for a sell-by date and only buy bags labeled for the current year.

Directions for use Tells when, how, and how much to apply for various types of plants, but use what you have learned about soil and plant needs to make smart choices beyond what the label suggests. Though it's cynical to say, it's in the fertilizer company's interest that you use more of its product. Base your actions on promoting soil fertility over simply feeding the soil.

**A fertilizer label tells you what
you need to know to choose and use it**

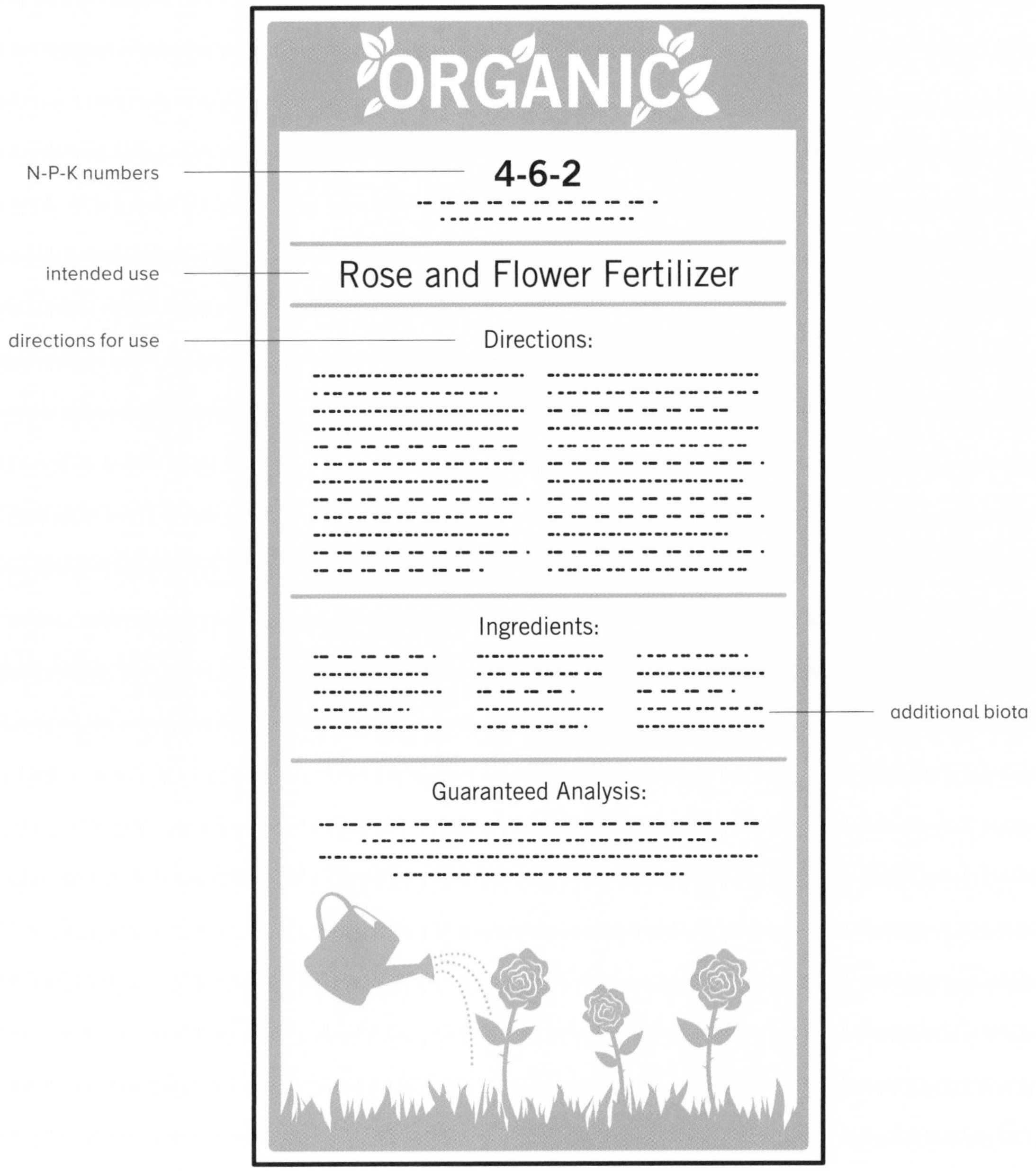

N-P-K numbers

intended use

directions for use

additional biota

ORGANIC

4-6-2

Rose and Flower Fertilizer

Directions:

Ingredients:

Guaranteed Analysis:

When to fertilize

The best time to fertilize your garden is when the plants need it most: in the spring when they are pushing new growth. This is especially true for all perennial plants, both woody and herbaceous. Each year deciduous plants make all new leaves, and evergreens add more to replace what was lost the previous year. Herbaceous plants start from the ground up, making entire new sets of shoots from overwintering roots, and annuals need extra nutrients to get them off to a good start. As a result, all plants benefit from extra nutrients during the first few months of the growing season.

Some plants also need season-long feeding. Edible gardens need steady replenishment of nutrients to produce successions of crops. Heavy feeders—like corn, melons, and squash—require abundantly fertile soils to make fruits. This starts with fertilizing the beds at the beginning of the season, before crops are planted. It's as simple as broadcasting a granular fertilizer directly over the soil and working it in with a rake. As each crop is harvested, do another feeding before the next crop goes in. The goal is to provide the right nutrients for each edible. For example, a high nitrogen fertilizer is best for leafy greens, like lettuce, spinach, and herbs. High phosphorus feeds should be used for plants that flower and fruit, like broccoli, tomatoes, and cucumbers. Potassium is good for root crops such as radishes, carrots, and beets. Summer annual flowers, either in beds or in pots, also benefit from season-long feeding, but only until they peak in late summer.

Landscape plants, container flowers, and lawns should not be fertilized after midsummer. Most growth has stalled by then, and perennial plants need to begin preparing for winter. A late-season feeding would encourage woody plants to sprout tender new growth, which might not have time to harden off before the autumn frosts arrive. Lawns too must go dormant. Fertilizing them as autumn approaches promotes new growth right when it's time to scale back. Fall applications of potassium or phosphorus to promote root growth can help new perennials or turf prepare for winter, but any fertilizer applied late in the season will ultimately leach away once active growth stops.

The gardener's footsteps might not be the best fertilizer, but the gardener's head, hands, and heart go a long way toward making something beautiful out of nature. Actions make gardens, and doing it right comes from experience as well as awareness. As we get to know our plants, our soil, and the garden as a whole, a fundamental evolution of our understanding about gardening unfolds. What was at first a simple plot of plants growing tentatively at our feet becomes an actual ecosystem created by and for us, a welcome attraction for the gardener and visitors alike.

How to Feed Plants in Spring

This method works wonders on any new landscape plantings or for existing plants that are performing poorly. Trees more than fifteen feet tall are too big to benefit from this type of feeding. Their roots should be well established by this point in their life and should be deep-root fed by a professional arborist instead. For all other plants, follow these three steps:

Step 1 During the first month of seasonal spring, determined by the climate where your garden is located (as late as May in Maine or as early as February in Florida), feed all your trees, shrubs, and herbaceous plants with a granular organic fertilizer. Use a basic blend with balanced N, P, and K and toss it at the root zone of each plant. A good rule of thumb for any fertilizer with N-P-K numbers in the single digits is to apply one cup for every foot of height of the tree or shrub. For herbaceous plants, sprinkle a ring of fertilizer around each plant as the shoots emerge.

Step 2 One month later, do it again. This application often coincides with spring mulching. If so, apply the fertilizer first, then mulch.

Step 3 One month later, do it again. Toss the fertilizer right on top of the mulch. The fertilizer will work its way down to the soil and the roots.

As the season unfolds, you will notice an improvement in the vigor of your landscape plants. They'll look lush, bloom profusely, and fruit prolifically. Neighbors might assume you're a gardening genius, but all you did was provide nutrients the plants needed. A few seasons of following this feeding cycle along with adding a topdressing of compost to the beds, and your plantings will be transformed.

vegetative propagation

Making Plants from Plant Parts

Plants want to grow. They want to spread and expand. Vegetative propagation takes advantage of this proclivity by tapping into a plant's growth force, the meristematic tissue. Any meristematic tissue will do: from a stem, a root, even a leaf. When looking to expand your garden, look no farther than the meristems of every plant you own. Learn how to harness this tremendous resource through vegetative propagation and a whole new world of gardening will open up to you.

Also called asexual propagation, this method of reproduction produces an exact clone of an existing plant. Two key benefits are genetic homogeneity and the fact that a clone reaches maturity in less time than it takes to start a plant from seed. Genetic identicalness can be desirable to perpetuate hereditary resistance to a pest or disease. In addition, consistent foliage, fruit, and flower shape, color, and size can be maintained.

The four primary vegetative propagation techniques are division, layering, cuttings, and grafting. Scientists also propagate plants from tissue culture, but you need a laboratory for that. Home gardeners rely primarily on division, layering, and cuttings.

The best method of vegetative propagation to use depends mostly on the plant in question. Many plants are super simple to divide, including daylilies, hostas, parsley, and chives. Others such as rhododendrons, hydrangeas, tomatoes, and spider plants lend themselves to layering. Plants best propagated from cuttings include forsythia, sedum, coleus, and peas. Basically, the right method will match the plant under consideration and the gardener's preference and skill. For example, daylilies are so easy to divide it would be foolish to bother with cuttings, and hydrangeas are so amenable to layering that any other method would add unnecessary effort.

Division

Division is the most straightforward method of vegetative propagation and the technique many gardeners learn first. The trick is to divide a single plant into two or more plants complete with roots, stems, and leaves. The leaves, actually, are optional, though it's best to include some foliage to kick-start growth through photosynthesis.

When dividing, you will probably want to dig and lift the entire plant out of the ground to get easy access to the roots. Spreading plants like bamboo, ajuga, or lawn grasses can be harvested in hunks without removing the entire plant. Plants with soft, fleshy roots are easily divided with a sharp spade. Plants with tougher roots require more serious tools. Hand pruners usually do the trick, but some plants require a saw. I once used a chain saw to divide some huge ornamental grasses with especially ornery root balls five feet in diameter.

What and when to divide

Herbaceous perennials are the most common candidates for division. Aside from propagation, most cultivated herbaceous perennials *must* be divided now and then to control their size or for rejuvenation: every four to five years for plants like daylily, phlox, and black-eyed Susan; every two to three years for astilbe, lamb's ears, and coreopsis; and every year for asters and blanket flower. Plants with taproots, like bleeding heart and false indigo, don't like to be divided and are best left undisturbed. Also refrain from dividing stressed or new plants. Divide only strong, healthy plants.

Gardener's Glossary

Sexual propagation is making plants by sowing seeds.

Asexual propagation is making more plants from plant parts.

Division is making two or more plants from one by dividing its roots, stems, and leaves into separate plants.

Layering is making one or more new plants by developing roots on a stem while the stem is still attached to the parent plant.

A **cutting** is a leaf, stem, or root of an existing plant used to make new plants.

Grafting is a horticultural technique used to join parts from two or more plants so that they grow as a single plant.

Perennials to Divide in Early Spring

agave

aster

bee balm

black-eyed Susan

bugbane

caladium

canna

Christmas fern

coneflower

dahlia

daylily

elephant ears

hosta

lamb's ears

monkshood

ornamental grasses

primrose

rhubarb

wild ginger

windflower

Perennials to Divide in Late Summer

arum

astilbe

bellflower

bergenia

brunnera

coral bells

coreopsis

creeping phlox

dianthus

foxtail lily

gayfeather

iris

lady fern

ligularia

lily of the valley

peony

poppies

rodgersia

sedges

Solomon's seal

When to do it depends on when the plant blooms. It's best to divide late-flowering plants in early spring and early-flowering plants in late summer. This makes sense. Dividing a spring bloomer, like brunnera, a few weeks before it flowers means missing out on its blooms for that season because digging, lifting, and slicing it apart will sap its strength. Better to divide it late in the season so it can emerge in the spring and flower unmolested. Conversely, a summer bloomer, such as coneflower, divided in spring has plenty of time to recover, set buds, and flower on schedule that same season.

A plant requires division when its center dies out and it starts growing into a ring. Iris and ornamental grasses do this. Hostas and peonies sometimes get so big they need to be diminished to fit their place in the garden. Division does the trick *and* provides a windfall of clones that can be planted elsewhere.

Some herbaceous perennials must be divided in order to survive. These are shallow-rooted species, like yarrow and aster. I learned this the hard way when I neglected to lift and divide a nifty sulfur-yellow yarrow I scored at a plant sale. The second season it was smaller, the third season tiny, and by the fourth year gone. I admit that after forgetting to divide it that first year, I decided to leave it alone on purpose just to see what would happen. What happened was that it disappeared.

Woody plants like Carolina allspice, rhododendron, and rugosa rose can also be divided but only when dormant—in earliest spring before bud break is best. Dividing woodies is tricky but doable. The more vigorous the shrub, the better the chances for success. If the shrub has any sentimental value to you whatsoever, such as being a gift from grandpa or a souvenir from a special trip, choose an alternative way to propagate it, like from a cutting or by layering.

How to divide, step by step

Step 1 Prepare each candidate for division ahead of time by watering as much as a day or at least an hour in advance. This helps hydrate the plant to prevent wilting, loosens the soil for digging, and makes it easier to keep the root ball intact as you lift it out of the ground.

Step 2 Dig the plant up using a long-handled fork or spade. Push into the ground in a complete circle around the plant several inches away from the crown (the area where the stem joins the root) to get the most roots possible. Be patient and loosen the roots all the way around with the fork instead of levering the plant out of the ground.

Step 3 Lift the clump out of the ground while holding the root ball with both hands. *Do not* yank it out by the shoots! Use hand pruners to clip any stubborn roots clinging to the earth under the root ball.

Step 4 With the clump lying on the ground and your foot on the fork or spade, divide the plant by slicing apart sections of the crown. Divide each clump into two, three, four, or more pieces. Use a pruner or saw to cut thick or woody roots.

Step 5 Select the divisions and untangle the roots below and the shoots above. The more roots and shoots each division has, the better its chances of survival and the sooner it will reach maturity again.

Step 1

Step 2

Step 3

Step 5

Step 4

Step 6 Plant the clones in prepared garden ground as you would a new plant from a pot. Treat them like new plants in every way, keeping them watered and mulched until they are fully established.

Step 6

Layering encourages the growth tissue in stems to form roots.

Plants Easily Propagated by Layering

azalea

blackberry

blueberry

bougainvillea

clematis

climbing rose

cotoneaster

daphne

grape

honeysuckle

hops

hydrangea

mock orange

philodendron

quince

raspberry

spirea

star jasmine

viburnum

wax myrtle

Layering

Layering makes use of a plant's meristematic tissue in a clever way. Burying a stem still attached to its parent plant encourages the growth tissue in the stem to form roots. Direct contact with soil or mulch wakes up latent growth tissue within the stem, and because it is underground it develops into roots instead of shoots. Remember, meristematic tissue can become any plant part. In this case, growth tissue in the stem becomes roots. It takes longer to make more plants by layering compared to other forms of vegetative propagation, but the actual work involved is a lot less laborious.

Layering should be started in spring to allow a full growing season for the new roots to form. The process is then completed the following spring, giving the plants a full growing season to establish before winter. Layering can be accelerated by slightly wounding the stem to expose the meristematic tissue before burying it.

Layering techniques

There are several layering techniques: simple, tip, serpentine, air, mound, and trench.

Simple is the perfect description of this layering technique. Simply bend the stem of a plant down to the ground so it's partially buried anywhere along its length and hold it in place with a pin, a stick, or even a heavy rock you find nearby. The tip of the stem will continue to grow and in time roots will form on the buried portion, which can be cut from the mother shrub and planted elsewhere to grow on its own. Simple layering is best for low-growing shrubs with flexible stems, like blueberry and bougainvillea.

simple

tip

serpentine

air

mound

trench

Choose from six layering techniques.

Tip layering works the same way as simple layering, but just the tip or apical meristem is buried. A year later, after a new shoot pokes out of the ground, it's ready to be severed from the mother plant and transplanted. Tip layering takes advantage of the natural reproductive activity of scrambling vines, like raspberry and blackberry.

Serpentine layering is a fancy version of simple layering. It looks a little like showing off but makes sense if there's just one good stem to work with—or if you want to work with only one stem—but you want to produce multiple clones. You bury sections of the stem but keep equal portions aboveground so shoots can form to support the new roots after transplanting. Plants with long, flexible stems like clematis, honeysuckle, and hops are excellent candidates for serpentine layering.

Air layering looks weird, but it works. This technique is useful for overgrown houseplants or woody outdoor plants with stiff stems you can't bend. In this technique the wound is key, as is the cleanliness of the rooting materials and the tools you use. The trick is to make a wound—a slit on herbaceous shoots and a ring on woody stems—to expose the growth tissue. Pack the area with water-soaked, coarse peat moss or shredded newspaper, cover it with plastic wrap, and tie it on so it's airtight. Roots should form in six to eight weeks in a warm, moist environment.

Mound layering is my favorite method because it's so easy. It's also especially useful when working with breakable multistem shrubs like spirea and mock orange. Simply bury the plant with a foot or two of soil or mulch, making certain the top leaves are exposed to the sun, and let it grow for at least a year. Come springtime, pull away the soil or mulch and check out all the new roots. Snip each stem just below the new mass of roots and plant it in a pot or in the ground. The mother plant will rejuvenate and can be layered again a few years later.

Trench layering looks a lot like plant abuse. Often used for orchard trees like apples and walnuts, the technique takes two years to complete but can produce many more clones than any of the one-year methods. Year one, plant the mother plant at a 45-degree angle and let it grow for a season. Year two, dig a trench beside the plant, make multiple wounds on the stems, then lay the plant down in the

trench and bury it. New shoots will form at each wound and can be dug, severed, and transplanted the following spring.

How to layer, step by step

Step 1 Evaluate the plant to determine which layering technique is best. If its stems are supple enough to bend down to the ground so contact is made with the soil, simple, tip, or serpentine layering should work. If the stems are stiff and upright, choose mound, air, or trench layering.

Step 2 Wound the portion of the stem to be buried (or sealed in plastic in the case of air layering). Make a cut just below a node to kick-start the growth tissue within.

Step 3 (optional) Hold open the wound with a toothpick or tiny pebble to keep the tissue exposed and encourage the meristem to form roots.

Step 4 Cover the stem with soil, mulch, or peat, pressing down to remove any air pockets. For simple, tip, or serpentine layering, pin the stem in place before burying it and/or place a large stone on top of the spot to secure it.

Step 5 Monitor the location for an emerging shoot and keep the soil moist for several weeks as the new roots develop.

Step 6 Dig up and cut the new shoot from the mother plant when it has several sets of new leaves and exhibits vigorous growth aboveground and belowground.

Step 7 Transplant the clone directly into a pot or the garden and treat it like a new planting by keeping the soil moist with supplemental watering and a light layer of mulch.

Layering isn't exactly effortless, but it sure is fun when it works. As a handy way to make more plants, it is invaluable for gardeners on a tight budget. Layering works well on every scale, from a few houseplants on a windowsill to institutional garden operations, and every garden in between. I can spot green-thumb gardeners when I see multiple layering projects in progress throughout their garden or in their glasshouse. The estates where I learned to garden had nursery areas set aside where plants were grown specifically for propagation—for layering as well as the next method of vegetative propagation, cuttings.

Step 1

Step 2

Step 4a

Step 4b

Step 5

Step 6

Step 7

Cuttings

Propagation from cuttings is exactly what the word describes: a gardener cuts off a piece of a plant and grows an entirely new plant from that part. The three primary types of cuttings are leaf, stem, and root. Leaf cuttings form roots and stems. Stem cuttings form roots and leaves. Root cuttings form stems and leaves. Sounds simple, but there is a trick to making each method work.

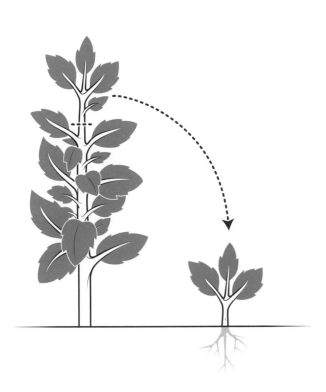

Propagation from cuttings is when a gardener cuts off a piece of a plant—a leaf, root, or stem—and grows a new plant from that part.

Plants That Are Easy to Propagate from Stem Cuttings

aster

azalea

boxwood

camellia

Christmas cactus

chrysanthemum

coleus

cypress

dracaena

fir

gardenia

geranium

holly

honeysuckle

hydrangea

lavender

penstemon

rose

rosemary

salvia

Plants That Are Easy to Propagate from Leaf Cuttings

African violet

dieffenbachia

echeveria

florist's gloxinia

jade plant

kalanchoe

peperomia

pineapple lily

plectranthus

rex begonia

sedum

snake plant

Plants That Are Easy to Propagate from Root Cuttings

aster

barrenwort

bleeding heart

cardoon

chrysanthemum

comfrey

golden rain tree

hollyhock

Joe Pye weed

Oregon grape

Oriental poppy

Osage orange

pasque flower

rose

rose of Sharon

sea holly

sundrop

trumpet vine

windflower

The purloined roadside cutting is an art and an adventure. I keep pruners, paper towels, plastic baggies, and a bottle of water in my car in case I spy something special growing in between public and private space where I might stop and swipe a snip.

Placing the meristematic tissue within a leaf or stem in direct contact with soil initiates formation of the two missing parts. Buried fleshy roots without shoots will respond by forming stems and leaves. Providing filtered light, consistent air and soil temperatures around 70 degrees F, and humidity levels around 70 to 80 percent helps ensure success. Use of a rooting hormone, especially with leaf cuttings, speeds up the process. With cuttings as with every other gardening task, the key to success is to treat the process as a fun learning experience. Dispel any fears of failure and let thoughts of making more plants for free inspire you.

How to propagate from stem or leaf cuttings, step by step

The easiest stem cuttings are softwood cuttings—taken from the early spring-green, nonwoody stem tips of a tree or shrub—or any stem of any herbaceous plant at any time. Leaf cuttings with petioles are most similar to stem cuttings. Thick leaves without petioles are easy too.

You'll get the best results if the cutting comes from a healthy plant and if you bear in mind that stem or leaf cuttings have no roots and that leaves are necessary to make roots. Remember, leaves harvest light energy and turn it into food used to grow roots, so keeping the leaves on a cutting alive is crucial. Start by trying a leaf cutting from a succulent plant like sedum, jade, or echeveria. Their fleshy leaves retain moisture and won't wilt for weeks without water. Stem cuttings of coleus, dracaena, and geranium are practically guaranteed to work, so also look to those as you learn.

Step 1

Step 2

Before you begin, sanitize your cutting tool to prevent the transfer of pathogens from the knife or pruners to the plant, or from plant to plant when taking multiple cuttings. Wipe the blade with rubbing alcohol or hold it over a flame for several seconds before each cut.

Step 1 Chose a strong top shoot from the plant's leader. Cut a half inch below a node to get a shoot that's four to six inches long with several sets of leaves. If you are out in the field or garden, wrap your cuttings in moist paper towels to keep them from drying out.

Step 2 At this point you can choose to make a leaf cutting or a stem cutting. For a leaf cutting, select a strong, clean, full-size leaf and cut it from the stem with the petiole intact. For a stem cutting keep the whole shoot but pinch off the bottommost leaves, leaving just a few at the top—enough to photosynthesize and power the formation of roots but not too many for the shoot to support without roots. Two or three leaves is enough. You might decide to use the pinched-off leaves for leaf cuttings and the remaining stem for a stem cutting.

Step 3

Step 4a

Step 4b

Step 3 (optional but recommended) Dip the end of each cutting in a rooting hormone powder to kick-start the growth of the meristematic tissue inside the stem or petiole. I use rooting hormone on leaf cuttings since they have less inherent growth tissue available than stems.

Step 4 Fill a seed tray or a small pot with moistened rooting medium: a mixture of equal parts sand and vermiculite. The mix should be heavy enough to hold the cutting

in place but light and well drained enough so it doesn't rot. Poke a hole in the medium with a chopstick or pencil and insert the stem of the shoot or the petiole of the leaf into the medium. Tamp it down gently to hold it in place.

Step 5 Set the cuttings in indirect light, like a north-facing window or outdoors in the shade. Direct sun will burn them and dry the rooting medium too quickly. Because cuttings have no roots, they can't absorb water from the

Step 5

Step 6

soil to stay alive, so the gardener must keep them from dry-ing out. If they dry, they die. Tent the plants using plastic baggies held on with rubber bands around the rim of the pot or tray. Make sure the baggie is easy to remove for daily visits with a spray bottle.

Step 6 Spritz the cuttings at least once a day if covered, three or more times a day if uncovered, depending on the ambient temperature and humidity. Warmer and drier conditions mean more spray visits. Pay attention to the rooting medium as well as the leaves. Keep them both moist but don't overdo it. If the mix stays soggy, the cut-tings will rot. Watch for new growth and monitor the leaves to be sure they aren't wilting or drying out. They should always look young and fresh.

Step 7 Roots should develop in six to eight weeks. To find out, gently tug on the leaf or stem. If it resists, there are

Step 7

roots. Grow it on another week or two so it gets stronger and ready for transplanting. Leaf cuttings will develop plantlets from the petiole after three or four months. You can carefully tease apart the entwined roots and plant each one separately for even more clones.

Step 8 When the stem cuttings form a second or third set of new leaves, they will have developed enough roots to allow for transplanting. Pot them up in a rich, well-drained potting mix in three-inch pots and let them grow on and get bigger. They should have lots of healthy roots before you plant them directly into the garden.

Step 8

How to Make Plants from Stem Cuttings the Lazy Way

If you don't feel ready to tackle the cuttings technique described step by step here, you can try the Lazy-Guy-Gardener method. It works especially well for plants with herbaceous stems, like coleus and geranium, but even woodies, especially dracaena, will work.

Snip off a stem with a few leaves intact, put the stem in a small glass of water or vase just like you do with cut flowers, and set it in a sunny window. In three to six weeks, roots will appear—without hormones, rooting medium, or misting. Just keep the water level high enough to cover at least half of the stem. I overwinter cuttings of my favorite annuals like this. It makes a nice display through the winter months and provides a fresh set of free plants first thing in the spring.

Cuttings in water make a nice window display and provide new plants for free.

How to propagate from root cuttings, step by step

Harvested from a vigorous parent plant, root cuttings become new plants when individual pieces of root sprout shoots. This technique can be used for herbaceous perennial plants as well as woody trees and shrubs, with just one slight difference between the two processes. Propagating plants from root cuttings takes a little added care and consideration, but the results are well worth the extra effort.

Take root cuttings only when the plant is dormant, in late fall or early spring. This minimizes the shock to the plant's system and maximizes the vitality of the roots, which have stored up sugars in preparation for dormancy. Choose plants with thick fleshy roots a half inch or more in diameter. Any section of root as thick as a pencil has enough stored food to develop a shoot and the requisite rootlets to support a clone.

Step 1 Lift herbaceous perennials out of the ground for easy access to the roots. Trees and shrubs are better left in place with a section of the roots excavated and exposed. Select lengths of root that are plump and firm, not hard or black. Look for long roots to get more pieces with less disturbance to the plant.

Step 2 Remove each length of root where it is attached close to the base of the plant. Collect no more than a quarter of the total root mass to make sure there's enough left to support the parent plant. Cut each length of root into two-to-six-inch pieces, with a straight cut on top and a diagonal cut on the bottom. This will help you identify the top later on when planting. Be sure to replant or rebury the exposed roots of the source plant.

Step 1

Step 2

Step 3 (woody root cuttings)

Step 3 for woody root cuttings Bundle woody root cuttings together with colored ribbon for identification. Cover the bundles with moist peat moss or sand inside a box and place the box in a refrigerator or any dark space maintained at 40 degrees F. This will keep them dormant until spring when the temperatures are above freezing and you can plant them directly into the garden.

Step 3 for herbaceous root cuttings Arrange herbaceous root cuttings two to three inches apart in a seed tray filled halfway with moistened soilless potting mix. Lay them flat and cover the pieces with enough mix to reach the top of the tray. Press down firmly on the surface with the palms of your hands to settle the mix around the roots. Put them under lights or near a bright window, keeping the rooting medium moist but not wet, and wait.

Step 4 In the spring, stored roots from woody plants can be planted directly in the ground by inserting each piece diagonal cut down. They will break dormancy and sprout when the temperatures warm with the season. Herbaceous perennial root cuttings stored indoors will sprout shoots in a few weeks but must be cold hardened before they can survive outside. Take the tray out during the day and in at night several times, or transfer it to a cold frame, to prepare the cuttings for harvesting. Allow the cuttings to grow on for several weeks outside in the trays. Wait until they develop several sets of new leaves before transplanting them into the garden. Keep the garden soil consistently moist until the clones are established in three or four weeks.

Step 3 (herbaceous root cuttings)

Step 4a

Step 4b

Grafting

If there's a propagation technique that approaches pure wizardry, it's grafting. Grafting is the process of joining together the growing parts of two plants to produce a single new plant. The union of a stem piece, called the scion, and a root piece, called the stock, is called a graft. Although grafting is not usually part of an amateur gardener's arsenal of propagation tricks, it's good to know the technique exists.

A common purpose of grafting is to grow a plant with a scion that possesses a desirable attribute the rootstock lacks, such as a weeping form, flowers of a certain color, or fruit with a distinct flavor. Sometimes the rootstock possesses the desired trait. One way home gardeners with limited space can have room for an orchard is to buy fruit trees grafted on dwarfing rootstocks. The dwarfing trait does not occur in the variety but in the rootstock to which it is grafted. For example, popular fruits like Anjou pear or 'Redhaven' peach, typically large orchard trees, can be grown as small specimens by grafting them on a dwarf rootstock. Rootstocks are also chosen for suitability to the soil and climate, or simply because they are already well established and ready to support a host of selective scions.

Nearly all fruit trees sold at nurseries are grafted because they do not come true from seed. The only way to be sure of getting the fruit you want is to make a clone, and grafting is the shortest path to a mature, fruiting specimen. You can see the graft point, an offset callused area, near the base of the trunk, right where it connects to the roots above the root flare. The graft area is the single most vulnerable part of a grafted plant and should be checked for rot or damage before you buy.

Scions can also be grafted directly to a tree trunk. Some years back I found a grower who made espaliered apple trees with six arms, each a different variety: Red Delicious, Macoun, Granny Smith, Golden Delicious, Empire, and McIntosh. The limbs were unique scions grafted onto the main trunk, which served as the stock. I bought all he had and used them in my garden designs for several years.

Making more plants though propagation is the best way to fill a garden. Use what you already own and know that a multitude of plants can also be had from fellow gardeners. My friend Jason throws a "dividing party" each spring. He marks all the herbaceous perennials needing division in his garden and sets spades nearby. Whoever digs, lifts, and divides a plant can take a piece home.

The joy of gardening is made manifest when the science of plants is married to the passion of a plant lover. The true gardener learns to love the effort it takes to create a garden from the ground up—to grow a tomato from seed or smell a flower on a shrub propagated from a cutting taken a decade earlier. Hands and plants work well together. Seeds want to start. Plants want to grow. It's that simple. Make more. Grow more. Garden more.

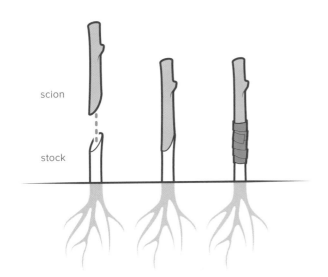

scion

stock

Grafting is an advanced propagation technique whereby the growing parts of two plants (the root piece or stock, and the stem piece or scion) are united to produce a new plant.

Apple tree with two scion cultivars—'Elstar' and 'James Grieve'—grafted onto one rootstock.

pruning

The Right Cut in the Right Place at the Right Time

Pruning is a skill that can be learned quickly but takes years to master. To become adept, you must know why you are pruning and understand that pruning stimulates growth. Whenever you prune, you redirect the flow of energy within a plant toward the development of desired plant parts, like foliage, flowers, and fruit, and sometimes even roots. Common gardening tasks like deadheading flowers and pinching new shoots are a form of pruning. They are part of the daily rhythm of routine gardening but adhere to the same principles as highly specialized forms of pruning such as espaliering, pleaching, pollarding, and coppicing. How to prune is all about technique and timing. Your first cuts can be intimidating, but like any acquired skill, pruning improves through practice.

Many gardeners don't prune because they don't know they're supposed to. On my first visit to client gardens, I usually find almost no proper pruning of ornamental trees and shrubs. I can tell when plants have been allowed to grow without the guidance of sensible cuts, but anyone can recognize when plants have been pruned right from the start. They look balanced and attractive. All woody trees and shrubs benefit from timely pruning, and herbaceous plants also profit from judicious snips. A fundamental understanding of pruning provides the confidence needed to make those first few pruning cuts, beginning a lifetime of the right cut in the right place at the right time.

Why Prune?

The purpose of pruning is threefold: to improve appearance, manage flowering and fruiting, and maintain health. In most cases a single pruning achieves all three goals, though different cuts produce different results.

Improve appearance

Proper pruning improves the appearance of plants. For example, fast-growing shrubs like winter honeysuckle and forsythia that tend to put out a tangle of shoots are transformed into vase-shaped specimens, or the asymmetrical

Gardener's Glossary

Espaliering is making cuts to train a plant to grow flat against a support such as a trellis or a wall.

Pleaching is weaving together the branches of adjacent trees to form a hedge or connected canopy.

Pollarding is removing the ends of branches on a tree to encourage new growth at the top of the canopy.

Coppicing is cutting a plant down to the ground to promote the growth of multiple stems.

Proper pruning results in a mature tree with a balanced appearance.

crown of a cherry tree is brought into balance. A spindly, unkempt shrub can be transformed into a full and bushy one, or an unruly tree can be shaped to fit its purpose and place.

Growth can be controlled by predicting how the meristematic tissue found in the stems, specifically at the nodes, will respond to each cut. Young herbaceous plants like basil or coleus grow bushier when their terminal buds are pinched off. This stimulates their axillary buds, making two or three new stems where there once was one. Pinching like this can be repeated several times during the season to promote lush plants.

Manage fruiting and flowering

The control of growth through pruning is naturally tied to flowering and fruiting. If a plant has more stems it will have more growth points, therefore the potential to produce more flowers and subsequently more fruit. Pruning cuts timed and designed to encourage and produce more stems and buds are made in late winter, while the tree or shrub is dormant. Herbaceous plants are cut back shortly after they emerge in the spring. The result in both cases is a resurgence of growth that forms more stems, hence more flower buds.

Flower buds can also be pruned. Deflowering a new plant its first year in the garden helps it establish because the energy that would have formed the flowers goes into making roots instead. Finished flowers can also be removed to promote a second or continual bloom. Removing a spent flower before it turns into a fruit and sets seeds sends a signal down the stem telling the plant to try again. Some herbaceous perennials like nepeta or shrubs like spirea faithfully repeat bloom when deadheaded, though the

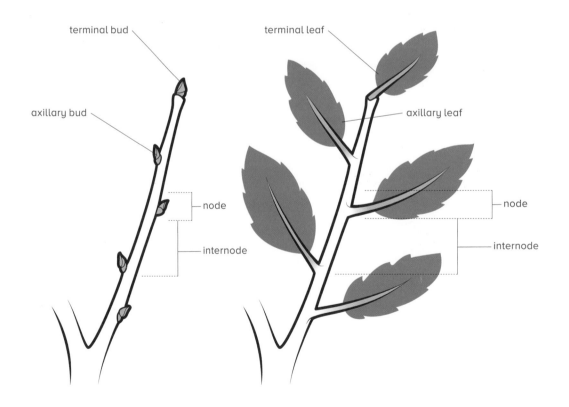

This illustration repeated from the first chapter is a reminder of how stems grow: from the terminal and axillary buds.

second flush never quite matches the first. Annuals like petunias and tender perennials like dahlias repeat bloom indefinitely when deadheaded.

Selective pruning can decrease the amount of fruit produced while improving fruit quality. Such is the case with orchard trees. A healthy apple tree left to itself in a sunny field will spread its branches wide and bloom profusely, but its apples will be inedible nubs. An orchard tree looks misshapen to the untrained eye, yet the contorted crown atop a fat trunk is designed to make good fruit. Thousands of buds have been removed to concentrate the tree's vitality into the production of fewer but better fruits. Every plant has a finite measure of vigor, energy it can expend in the production of fruit and flowers. A mature, orchard-pruned apple tree will produce a thousand edible apples instead of making five thousand crummy ones.

Maintain health

Proper pruning also helps maintain plant health and can rejuvenate a weak or failing shrub. Branches on woody plants sometimes break or inexplicably die. Because such damaged or dead limbs are a gateway for pests and disease, they should regularly be removed from trees and shrubs. The old stems on roses, for example, often die after a harsh winter, but fresh green canes soon replace them. The old wood should be cut out, not left to rot on the plant.

Any shrub can lose vigor over time, causing old stems to produce fewer leaves and fail to flower. That's when rejuvenation pruning is required. When old stems are removed, energy from the roots causes sprouting of fresh young shoots capable of making enough leaves to power the formation of flowers. It's literally out with the old wood and in with the new wood, resulting in more productive plants.

When to Prune

Like every new gardener, I made mistakes and learned lessons the hard way when I was just starting out. I cringe when I recall pruning a large limb from a mountain ash while it was actively fruiting. The limb obstructed a new path, so I summarily removed it from the tree. The

Old rose canes should be cut out after a harsh winter.

resulting wound hemorrhaged sap like blood from a severed artery. Within the week, the tree was wilting and the leaves were falling off. Weakened, it did not survive the winter. Since then I've been careful to time my cuts based on the season and stage of growth of the plant.

Following are some tips about when to prune various types of plants.

Deciduous trees Whenever dormant. Early or late winter is best to avoid stress to the plant, excess bleeding of sap, and leaf loss. Never prune fruit or other deciduous trees in early autumn. Stimulated new growth may not have time to harden off (acclimate to harsher conditions) before winter frosts set in.

Flowering shrubs *Never* when in bloom. The general rule is to prune after flowering, though there are exceptions. Plants that bloom on "new wood" (stems made that season), like smooth hydrangea, can be pruned in spring before flowering and will still bloom that season.

Coniferous evergreens When new growth is still green in early spring. Only cut the soft new shoots. The meristematic tissue in old growth on most conifers will not respond when the stem is pruned. Soft-needled conifers like yew, hemlock, and arborvitae are exceptions and should be pruned as broadleaf evergreens.

Broadleaf evergreens After the new growth has hardened off. This is when fresh, soft foliage darkens to match last year's leaves, typically by late spring. Never prune in early autumn. Stimulated new growth may not have time to harden off before winter frosts set in.

Herbaceous perennials Before flowering, to control their size and make them bushy. Tall perennials won't flop if cut by half in early spring. However, this will delay their flowering period by two or more weeks. Prune in midsummer to rejuvenate ragged plants. Cut catmint, sage, and daylily, among others, down to the ground to promote fresh foliage and a second bloom.

Basic Pruning Tools

The most important thing about pruning tools is to keep them sharp and clean. Dull blades make work more difficult, resulting in jagged cuts and tears that look bad and leave wounds susceptible to pests and disease. It's smart to sterilize your blade with disinfecting wipes or a cloth soaked in rubbing alcohol when moving from plant to plant. This prevents the inadvertent transfer of pathogens. At a minimum, always clean, sharpen, and sterilize your tools after each pruning session so they are ready when you need them.

Hand pruners are the most important tool a gardener owns and should always be with you in the garden. They are perfect for deadheading, deadleafing, and cutting woody stems as thick as a pencil. Invest in a top-quality pair that can be dismantled, cleaned, and repaired.

A few sharp tools make pruning easier. From left to right: pruning saw, shears, hand pruners, pole saw, bow saw, loppers.

Pruning stimulates growth, and plants needs nutrients to power that growth, so always feed your plants after you prune. Use what you know about fertilizers and apply nitrogen for foliage and phosphorus for flowers.

Loppers are for cutting branches larger than a pencil but no more than two inches in diameter. When used on limbs larger than that, the result is a jagged cut or damage to the tool. The longer the handle, the bigger the branch the loppers can tackle. Invest in a top-quality pair that can be dismantled, cleaned, and repaired.

Pruning saws are for cutting branches too big for loppers and up to six inches in diameter, depending on your strength and stamina. Razor teeth designed to cut on the push and the pull get the job done fast. An eighteen-inch fixed blade in a scabbard is best, but small folding saws are handy for impromptu jobs.

Shears come in all shapes and sizes, but they are meant for one thing—quickly cutting large swaths of thin or soft stems. Use them for hedging, to cut back ornamental grasses, or to deadhead masses of perennials. The most important trait in shears is weight. Lighter is better, especially if you have a hundred feet of hedge to clip. Power shears are for contractors who maintain thousands of feet of hedge each year. Gardeners should use manual shears. They slow the process, which produces better results.

Bow saws are a type of pruning saw designed for limbs greater than six inches in diameter. Their thin, replaceable blades with coarse teeth make short work of soft woods, like pine and poplar, and cut easily through dead wood.

Pole saws do what loppers and pruning saws do, but with an extended handle to prune trees up to fifteen feet tall. Anything taller requires ladders, bravery, and balance. The lopper mechanism is attached to a rope pulled to make the cut. The saw is attached to the end. Top quality is the way to go to avoid the frustration of flimsy poles and weak fasteners.

Chainsaws are the ultimate weapon when it comes to removing limbs. A small one is best for pruning. Big ones are for felling trees. Some chainsaws come attached to poles, making them ultra-useful and equally dangerous. Electric-powered chainsaws work well but are as dangerous as gas-powered saws.

Basic Pruning Cuts

There are two primary pruning techniques for woody plants: heading back and thinning out. Heading cuts are made above a growth point, or node, resulting in bushier growth; they are perfect for sheared hedges, like privet or camellia. Shearing is akin to making dozens of heading cuts at once and works best on stems with short internodes. Thinning cuts are made below a node and just above the juncture of a lateral stem, resulting in growth that extends outward. Thinning cuts create open canopies, allowing sunlight and air to enter the crown. The result is a well-formed tree or shrub.

Always consider the long-term consequences when you prune. If the tips of a woody plant are headed back, it must be pruned in the same fashion each year to check excessive growth stimulated by previous cuts. It is possible to restore it to its natural form, but only after several years of well-placed thinning cuts. Drastic heading cuts can irreparably distort a tree's natural form. So can removing the lower limbs. Called limbing up, it's often done to increase airflow and sun exposure beneath a canopy. A better way to achieve that is to make thinning cuts that open the canopy. This calls to mind something an old-time arborist once told me: "A canopy tree is pruned correctly if a bird can fly through it." Remember that and you won't go wrong.

Proper pruning requires careful cuts, not haphazard hacks. When cutting above a node, make the cut on a diagonal slanting away from the node, leaving a small amount of stem to support the new terminal bud. In this case, water runs off easily and the wound heals quickly. If the diagonal is in the wrong direction, water will run onto the bud and cause rotting. If the cut is too close to the bud, the bud may die. If it's too flat, it holds water, which may rot the bud. If too much of a stub is left, the wound won't heal properly and infection may occur, leading to dieback. If the diagonal is too long, infection can easily enter the wound.

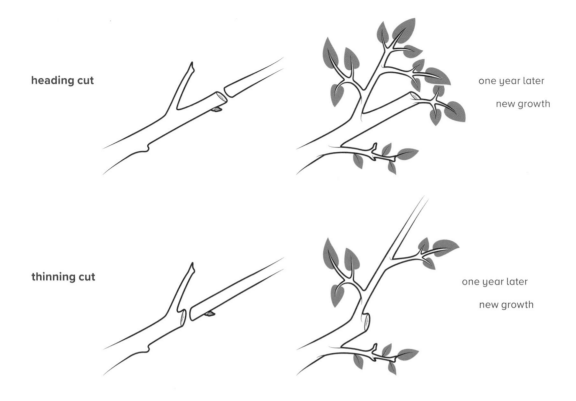

heading cut

one year later

new growth

thinning cut

one year later

new growth

Heading and thinning cuts have different effects on subsequent growth.

Gardener's Glossary

Deadheading is removing spent flowers to promote a second or continual bloom.

Deadleafing is removing old or damaged leaves to improve a plant's appearance.

Heading back is making pruning cuts above a growth point, or node, resulting in bushier growth.

Thinning out is making pruning cuts below a node and just above the juncture of a lateral stem, resulting in growth that extends outward.

A great way to practice proper cuts is to tend hybrid tea roses. They need constant pruning, yet their vigorous growth quickly erases mistakes, while their menacing prickles encourage thoughtful consideration of each cut. My own crash course in proper pruning cuts took place in a rose garden with more than a hundred hybrid teas. I started out gloveless, forcing myself to execute each cut with consummate care among the prickles. I can only imagine what my employers thought as they heard my intermittent yelps emanating from behind the garden wall.

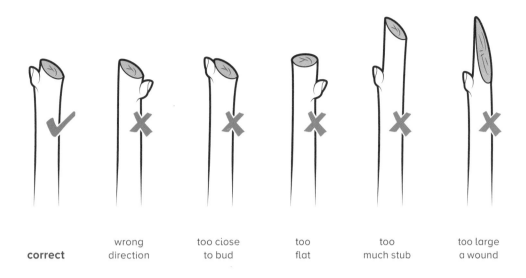

| correct | wrong direction | too close to bud | too flat | too much stub | too large a wound |

A pruning cut above a node must be made carefully on a diagonal.

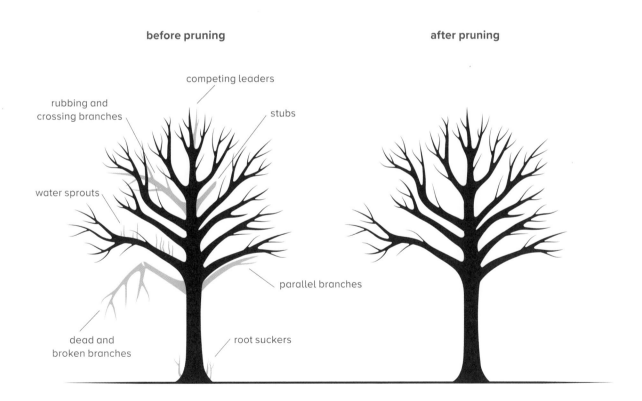

before pruning

after pruning

competing leaders

rubbing and crossing branches

stubs

water sprouts

parallel branches

dead and broken branches

root suckers

Know what to prune before starting to make cuts.

Pruning Deciduous Trees

Deciduous trees do us the favor of losing all their leaves so that we can assess their structure and easily see how it can be improved. They should be pruned when dormant to avoid stressing them, ideally in early or late winter.

What to prune

To properly prune deciduous trees, you need to know what to prune.

Dead and broken branches and stubs must be removed to prevent pests and disease from entering the plant's vascular system through ragged wounds. A clean cut at the trunk decreases the chances of infection or infestation.

Rubbing and crossing branches in time can damage the bark, allowing for pests and disease to infiltrate. If ignored, limbs can become deformed, creating weak spots prone to breakage. The gardener must pick a winner, keeping one branch and losing the other.

Parallel branches become rubbing branches, but long before that the top branch will shade out the lower one and weaken it. Remove one or the other to open up the crown, allowing sunlight to reach as many leaves as possible.

Competing leaders often form a weak central crotch on the trunk and should be removed to balance the tree's overall form. Pruning to one leader is the single most recognizable difference between a pruned tree and trees in the wild.

Water sprouts shoot vertically from major limbs, destroying the form of the canopy as well as shading branches below. Left unchecked, they will grow into and rub against nearby branches.

Root suckers turn a tree into a shrub by emerging at its base and surrounding the trunk. Often resulting from disturbance to the root zone, they can be limited by building a large mulch ring around the tree (but not touching the trunk).

To find out if a branch is truly dead in late winter or early spring before the leaves have emerged, scrape the thin bark of a slim twig with a fingernail and look for green tissue underneath. If it's green, it's alive. If it's brown, it's dead. Scrape again further down the branch until you find green to determine how much to prune. If there is no green tissue along the entire branch, do the test on the trunk of the plant, as the plant may have died completely.

How to Choose Between Branches

When choosing between rubbing, crossing, and parallel branches, keep the branch with the strongest crotch. The smaller the angle between limb and trunk the weaker the connection, making it more likely the branch will break under stress. Trees with weak wood and V-shaped crotches, like ornamental pears, are often demolished by heavy snows or windstorms. Strong wood, like oak, with U-shaped crotches can withstand tremendous strain without breaking.

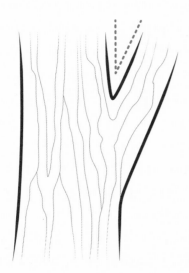

V-shaped crotch

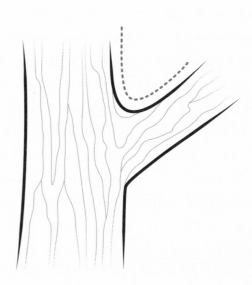

U-shaped crotch

The closer the crotch angle to 90 degrees, the more trustworthy the limb. Keep branches with U-shaped crotches and prune out those with V-shaped crotches.

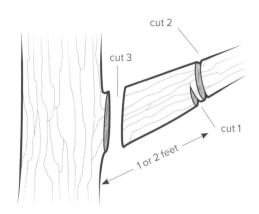

Make three cuts to remove limbs larger than three inches in diameter.

The three-cut method to prune a large limb

When removing any limb with a saw, use the three-cut method to avoid torn bark and jagged stubs.

Cut 1 Partially cut upward into the branch a third to halfway through. This prevents the bark from ripping off below the intended cut.

Cut 2 Saw downward all the way through the branch two or three inches out from cut 1. This removes most of the weight of the limb.

Cut 3 Saw downward all the way through the branch just outside the branch collar, where the branch widens to meet the trunk. With the outer weight removed, a sharp saw will make a clean, complete cut without tearing the bark.

Allow pruning wounds to close on their own. At one time it was common to slap pruning sealer on cuts, but research has shown that this can trap pathogens inside, whereas the sap that seeps from the wound keeps it clean and helps form a callus.

A pruning wound if left alone will close on its own.

Call a pro to prune mature trees or shrubs more than fifteen feet tall. Ever since the day I nearly dropped a thirty-foot honey locust on my friend's mom's house, my limit is set at the reach of my pole pruner. Anything above that is best done with a lift or bucket truck by a licensed arborist. Use what you have learned about pruning to interview potential arborists, and watch them while they work. If they use the three-cut method, you're in good hands.

Getting young trees off to a good start

Most young trees need pruning to get them off to a good start. After their first dormant season, prune all dead wood, and do this after every subsequent dormant season. Following their third full season in the garden, when their roots are fully established, assess the tree's branching structure. Now is the time to prune to a central leader if there is more than one, and remove crossing, rubbing, or parallel branches with thinning cuts to establish evenly spaced lateral branches. This will open the canopy, balance the shoots with the roots, and set the tree on course for a lifetime of proper pruning.

Pruning fruit trees

Late winter pruning is required for all productive fruit trees. Thinning cuts should be made to shape the crowns while the trees are dormant. Pome fruits, such as apples and pears, form on spurs, short branchlets with plump buds growing from mature fruiting branches. These spurs can be thinned to five to six inches apart so the fruit will have room to mature properly. This also concentrates the tree's energy into producing fewer but better fruits. Stone fruits—like peaches, apricots, and cherries—work the same way. Once established, they grow rapidly, requiring

that as many as 25 percent of the existing branches be removed at the beginning of each season, paying close attention to keeping ample fruiting spurs and plump buds.

Pruning Evergreen Trees and Shrubs

The two categories of evergreens, conifer and broadleaf, require different pruning protocols.

Conifers with stiff needles, like pine and spruce, should be pruned infrequently or not at all, the removal of dead-wood being the sole exception. Their ultimate size and shape can be molded by trimming the soft spring growth at the tips, called candles, but these cuts must be made individually with hand pruners. Never shear a spruce! On the other hand, soft-needled conifers, like hemlock and yew, respond well to early summer shearing.

The fresh growth of broadleaf evergreens, like rhododendron, holly, and laurel, must harden off before pruning takes place. New growth transforms from light green and pliable in early spring to dark and sturdy by early summer. That's when they are ready to be pruned with heading cuts to keep them bushy. For large plantings or a severe look, shears can be employed.

Pruning Deciduous Shrubs and Herbaceous Perennials

Almost all herbaceous plants and certain shrubs can be rejuvenated by cutting their stems nearly to the ground. Lilacs especially like it. In fact, rejuvenation pruning is part of the regular maintenance of many plants.

The first time I witnessed a rejuvenation pruning first-hand, I was horrified. A landscape crew with chainsaws invaded the backyard of my rental house in Wisconsin one spring and hacked to the ground a lilac hedge separating our yard from the neighbor's. As the crew remorselessly hauled the brush away, leaving a row of four-inch stumps, I stepped outside to confront them. "It's a rejuvenation

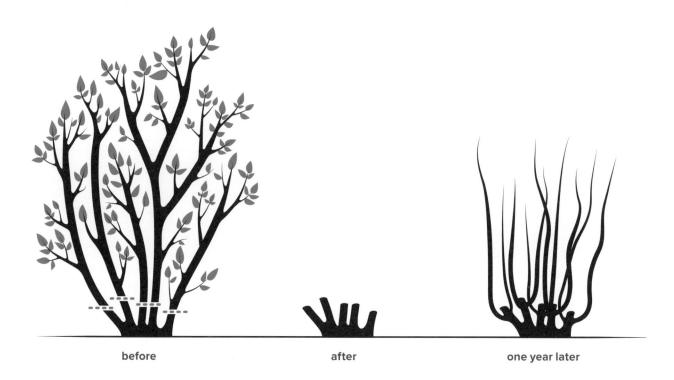

before **after** **one year later**

Cutting back a shrub hard results in a healthier, more compact plant a year later.

prune, buddy," the foreman explained. "It will grow back in no time, bigger and better than ever." I doubted him then but later learned he was right. By the end of August, the hedge was five feet tall, healthy and strong.

Plants that are leggy, with long, weak stems, will rebound after a severe trim, but not in just any season. Spring is the best time for a rejuvenation pruning, and it will only be successful if the plant's roots are strong. A weak plant is more likely to die if cut back hard, so in this case perform a multiyear rejuvenation pruning instead.

In midsummer, you can tidy up a tired-looking flower garden by removing spent blooms and damaged leaves. Called deadheading and deadleafing, this simple gardening task is as valuable as the most sophisticated pruning. An hour of clipping and trimming readies the plants for an attractive end to the season.

How to Do a Multiyear Rejuvenation Pruning

The shocking sight of a large shrub cut all the way to the ground can be avoided by employing a three-year sequence of rejuvenation cuts. This technique accomplishes the same thing spaced over time for a less drastic look.

first year   second year   third year

Multiyear rejuvenation pruning reduces the shock of seeing a large shrub cut to the ground.

Year 1 Cut back one-third of the stems to ground level.

Year 2 Cut back another third of the original older stems to ground level. Thin young branches to shape the plant.

Year 3 Cut back the remaining third of the original older stems to ground level. Thin young branches to shape the plant.

Shrubs That Respond Well to Rejuvenation Pruning

abelia
beautyberry
butterfly bush
ceanothus
crape myrtle
dogwood
forsythia
heather
honeysuckle
lilac
ninebark
osmanthus
pittosporum
privet
pussy willow
quince
raspberry
rugosa rose
spirea
viburnum

Herbaceous Perennials to Deadhead

agapanthus
astilbe
bellflower
bergenia
cardinal flower
catmint
coral bells
coreopsis

Herbaceous Perennials to Deadhead (*continued*)

cranesbill
crocosmia
daylily
delphinium
dianthus
gayfeather
hellebore
hosta
iris
lavender
ligularia
lupine
meadow sage
peony
rodgersia
scabiosa
speedwell
spiderwort

Shrubs to Deadhead

andromeda
azalea
butterfly bush
camellia
choisya
crape myrtle
deutzia
forsythia
fothergilla
hebe

Shrubs to Deadhead *(continued)*

hydrangea

lilac

oleander

rhododendron

rose

rose of Sharon

smokebush

spirea

summersweet

tree mallow

Deadheading, or removing spent blooms, tidies up the garden.

Pruning Vines

The goal when pruning vines is to prevent rampant growth from smothering adjacent plants or causing damage to structures. Different varieties respond to different cuts.

Twining vines, like clematis, honeysuckle, and passion flower, develop scraggly bottoms when neglected. The right cut is to prune the vine close to the ground and let it start fresh each season from increasingly vigorous roots.

Clinging vines, like climbing hydrangea, trumpet vine, and ivy, gradually creep up a chimney, façade, or fence, sending out new branches that lay claim to more territory each year. The best thing to do with clingers is to edit the new stems, thinning them out to promote good air circulation while guiding their growth in a preferred direction, such as along the top of a wall or away from windows and gutters.

Like all forms of knowledge, our gardening knowledge evolves. Expertise is built on early experiences, much like the first pruning cuts to a new tree initiate its development from an unremarkable sapling to a stately specimen. You will prune successfully when you understand the fundamental reasons for each type of cut and the expected responses of the plants to be pruned. Online research works, and there are excellent books on pruning available. I still carry a pruning manual in my work truck—just in case.

What you learned here is only the beginning, but that's the fun of gardening. My advice is to practice on plants that grow fast and respond well to pruning, such as tea rose, mock orange, and spirea. This will build your confidence, increase your understanding of how energy flows inside each plant, and teach you that every cut you make influences growth—of the plant, and of you, the gardener.

weeds, pests, and diseases

Working with the Bad, the Good, and the Ugly

Gardening is a balancing act between nature's limits and the gardener's desires, between the bane and the beauty. If gardening were easy, there would be no sense of accomplishment when success is achieved. In previous chapters you learned how to promote the roots and the shoots to grow happy, hearty plants, but now we come to the darker side of gardening. Weeds, pests, and occasional disease issues arise in every garden, no matter how impeccably cared for. The right approach is to work proactively to prevent these problems, and when trouble does strike, to eschew simple fixes that may or may not work, or that may actually make matters worse. A little know-how can go a long way toward helping you choose safe and smart solutions.

Weed Control: A Weed Is an Unloved Plant

No plant is inherently evil. Dandelions and crabgrass aren't out to wreck our lawns on purpose. Weeds are just opportunists. They find an empty niche in the landscape and fill it; they locate a chink in the horticultural armor of a garden and exploit it. It harkens back to what you learned earlier: plants want to grow. While gardeners find ways to assist the plants they love, weeds succeed on their own.

My favorite definition of a weed is "an unloved plant." When what was once a prized herb in time becomes a scourge, we ascribe the experience to youthful folly and move on, sadder but wiser. Many plants fall out of favor, sometimes for very good reasons, such as invasives that upset the natural balance of an ecosystem. Others are deemed unacceptably ugly by arbiters of good taste. Whatever the case may be, many plants are commonly identified as weeds, though we don't always know them when we see them.

Weeds are unloved for a few reasons:

- Weeds are messy. While some weeds are individually beautiful, collectively weeds lend an untidy appearance to a garden. Weeds grow wherever they can take hold, disrupting the order of thoughtful plantings.

- While some gardeners like things messy and think a pretty weed deserves a second look, the fact remains that weeds take nutrients and water from the soil. Weeds are greedy usurpers that deplete garden resources, limiting what's available to plants we want to grow.

- Weeds grow fast and ignore all boundaries between plants. They crowd and shade desirable plants, growing so big they push them aside, or scramble to steal their sun. Left unchecked, weeds can take over a garden in a single season, destroying years of effort.

Two types of weeds: seed and root

Seed weeds propagate predominantly by seed. Fast-growing annuals, they shoot up suddenly, flower, and set new seed,

Weeds make a garden look untidy while taking nutrients and water from the soil and crowding desirable plants.

sometimes in the course of a single week. You know them when you pull them. They have weak roots and pull easily because most of their energy goes into making shoots, flowers, and ultimately seeds. Once removed they are gone for good, but if they finish flowering and set seed, thousands more potential weeds lie in wait in the soil. Never let a weed set seed. The prime rule of weeding is: if you see a weed in bloom, pull it there and then.

Root weeds propagate insidiously underground. While they also flower and can spread from seed, like dandelions do, these perennial weeds send up shoots from spreading roots. Much more difficult to eradicate than seed weeds, root weeds are hard to pull, and when they do come out the root often breaks, leaving pieces in the soil that will

Weed Mimicry

Is it a cultivated species or a weed mimic? Snow-on-the-mountain (green-and-white leaves) and blackberry (green leaves) look very similar.

All gardens are filled with interesting sights, but a most curious marvel is when a weed mimics another plant. The first time I saw it, I was a new gardener and didn't believe my eyes. Since then I've witnessed it many times and still find it uncanny. What typically occurs is that in well-established gardens where many generations of weeds have come and gone, a weed matching the appearance of a desired plant finally arrives. Often the wild cousin of the plant it sidles up to, with similar leaf shape, size, and arrangement, it gives the gardener pause before pulling it—or eludes the gardener's weeding rounds altogether.

Garden plants and their weedy mimics include morning glory and bindweed; lamb's ears and common mullein; marigold and ragweed seedlings; and marsh marigold and lesser celandine.

propagate. Rototilling root weeds has disastrous results. Chopping them into pieces creates thousands of root cuttings, which become thousands more new weeds.

When and how often to weed

There are cool season weeds and warm season weeds. Cool season seed weeds germinate in early spring. Once the soil warms up they stop, and the warm season weeds kick in. The weeding season starts in spring and as soil temperature changes, different weeds cycle through. Populations of seed weeds germinate in sequence, so once they appear and are pulled, they don't come back in large numbers until their preferred growing conditions return. Any seed weed can appear sporadically throughout the season but never in numbers comparable to its first wave. Root weeds emerge based on their seasonal preference of cool or warm and often persist all season long, spreading through the garden underground.

The best way to keep weeds at bay is to weed every week during the growing season, from the time you spot the first interloper until freezing temperatures shut them down. Not every root weed can be completely removed, and the cycle of seed weeds will keep coming, but weekly weeding

Keep root weeds out of your compost pile. A small composter can be overrun with root weeds that propagate instead of decomposing in the pile, so it's best to dispose of them differently. You can compost the shoots but consign the roots to the trash or a larger composting system, like community windrows or large heaps. Seed weeds are safe for composters because their roots won't propagate and the heat generated during decomposition ruins the viability of their seeds.

Gardener's Glossary

Seed weeds are unwanted annual plants that propagate from seeds naturally dispersed throughout the soil in a garden.

Root weeds are unwanted perennial plants that propagate from the roots of existing weeds already in the garden.

Herbicides are substances that are toxic to plants, used to kill unwanted vegetation.

Personal protective equipment (PPE) is the clothing, such as goggles, gloves, and masks, worn to protect the gardener from toxic chemicals.

will limit the quantity of water and nutrients they steal from the soil and keep them from crowding other plants. As the season progresses and desirable plants fill in the gaps, fewer and fewer weed seeds will germinate. By the middle of summer, the weeds will be under control and time spent weeding will decrease significantly.

Tools for weeding

My first experience battling weeds took place when I was a teenager and my mom decided I would help her grow a vegetable garden. I had no idea what I was doing, and unfortunately, neither did she, so I can't say we were very successful. When I landed my first professional gardening gig I approached weeding with a bit more aplomb, arming myself with a few key tools I still use to fight weeds today. Though many weeding gimmicks are available, here's all you really need:

Gloves Always wear gloves to protect your hands from drying out or touching something you don't want to touch, like poison ivy or prickers. I use goatskin gloves for supple but solid protection against thistles and thorns, and nitrile-palmed cloth gloves for delicate hand weeding.

Stirrup or loop hoe This is the end-all, be-all tool for uprooting weeds. A sharpened, looped blade on a hinge at the end of a long handle makes slicing through weed roots a breeze when you are attacking a large patch. It also works dexterously within beds, knocking down young weeds while sparing good plants.

Soft rake A long-handled soft-tined rake is the most efficient way to gather masses of weeds into piles for quick pickup.

Bucket I prefer a five-gallon pickle bucket with a wire handle. In a pinch I'll commandeer a discarded plant liner from a store-bought shrub to drag along and fill with weeds as I go.

Wheelbarrow Keep a wheelbarrow or cart nearby to dump the weeds from the collecting bucket into when it gets full. Then use the wheelbarrow to transport the day's weeds to the compost pile or trash.

Pump sprayer These are handy when you want to strike pernicious or noxious weeds, like poison oak or dandelions, with an herbicide.

How to weed

"There's no such thing as a Garden of Eden because there's no such thing as a Garden Without Weeding." That's a motto I made up to drive home the point that if you want to have a garden, you have to weed. Though weeding is unavoidable, you can choose from several different techniques.

Hand weeding is the safest and smartest way to weed. Pull weeds when they are small. Once they grow large, their roots will resist. Small weeds also mean less to haul away and less water and nutrients stolen from the soil. Avoid daytime heat and direct sun when hand weeding. Start at dawn or dusk, when the temperatures are cooler. If you must work during midday, follow the shade, weeding under trees or in the shadow of structures. Pulling weeds is easier if the soil is moist, another reason to weed in the morning before the dew dries. Plan a weeding session for the day after it rains or water the garden several hours beforehand.

Hand weeding is best done when the weeds are small and the soil is moist.

Hoeing and cultivating is a great way to remove shallow-rooted weeds from large areas, but stay clear of shallow-rooted trees and shrubs, like maples and rhododendrons. A sharp metal tool will damage their roots. Dry conditions are best for this method. If it's wet, a hoe will work the soil into a muddy mess. Big weeds can be knocked down with a hoe, but it's better to attack them when they are small and easily uprooted. Small seed weeds can stay where they lie to compost on the ground, but big weeds should be raked out and tossed onto the compost pile.

Mulching is a weed control but only for weeds that start from seeds. Root weeds will grow right through mulch, and so will seed weeds that have already sprouted. That's why mulch works as a weed control only if it's applied before seed weeds germinate. In new landscape beds mulch is used to delay weeds, not prevent them. In edible

How to Tell If It's a Weed You're Pulling

If you are unsure whether what you are pulling is a weed, ask: Did I plant it? If not, it's a weed. If you can't remember, check if it's growing in an odd spot or too close to a known plant. If it is, it's probably a weed. Are many specimens of the same plant growing randomly all around? If so, it's either a weed or a garden plant that has self-sown.

Give it a tug. If it has weak roots and pops out easily, it's most likely a seed weed. If it has strong roots, it's probably a perennial flower or a root weed. Check around the soil and look for telltale signs of potting mix from a store-bought plant. If you find bits of what looks like Styrofoam (perlite) around the roots, it's probably a store-bought plant, not a weed. Look for a plant label. I like to bury the label next to the root ball when I plant. If you find a label that matches the plant, it's definitely not a weed.

A stirrup hoe makes quick work of slicing through weed roots.

beds, a mulch like straw can be used to suppress weeds while providing all the other benefits mulch brings.

Chemical weed controls, or herbicides, are useful where hand weeding is prohibitive, cultivation is difficult, and mulching impractical. There are two types of chemical herbicides: selective and nonselective. For example, crabgrass killer is a selective herbicide. When applied to lawn it only kills crabgrass, not turf. Nonselective herbicides don't care what they kill. Whatever they touch, they hurt. The active ingredient is sprayed on the leaves, where it is absorbed, and travels down the vascular system to kill the roots. When the roots die, the shoots die.

There are products made from natural ingredients, like clove or garlic oil, that work like chemical herbicides, but always remember that even eco-friendly herbicides are nonselective and will kill whatever plants they touch. They also tend to be less effective than chemically manufactured weed killers.

Some alternative ways to kill weeds include the following:

- For random, tenacious weeds, pour boiling water on them from a teakettle. This will wreak havoc on their cellular structure and kill them quickly.

- A mixture of a gallon of vinegar with a cup of table salt and a teaspoon of liquid dishwashing soap sprayed on a weed, or any plant, will kill it. It will also kill the soil, so use it judiciously.

- You can use a gas torch or flame weeder to reduce weeds to cinders, but use it only on those that grow in gravel or between stones far away from the house, never near mulch or other flammable materials.

- Corn gluten meal is an eco-safe weed control that works against seed weeds by disrupting their root growth after they germinate.

Solving Pest Problems

When garden pests are mentioned, we tend to think about insects—bugs that crawl or fly and feed upon our plants. They may visit briefly, or they may move in, laying eggs on roots, stems, or leaves. Many insects are easy to spot because of their size or brazen appearance, like beetles,

How to Apply Chemical Herbicides—If You Must

There are real concerns about the use of herbicides and their long-term effects on the soil and the gardener. If plants eat soil and we eat plants, whatever is in the soil ends up in us. If you do choose to use chemical herbicides, follow the label as if it were the letter of the law—because it is. Careless use of herbicides is dangerous to people, animals, and the environment.

The purchaser of a chemical herbicide (or pesticide) assumes responsibility for the proper use and/or disposal of the product according to the rules and regulations written on the label. The moment the bottle is opened, the label becomes a legally binding contract between the gardener and the chemical company, with language that limits the company's liability for negligent use or unintended results. Always wear personal protective equipment and use the chemical sparingly, because it will have detrimental effects on the living ingredients in the soil and in you.

Gardener's Glossary

Integrated pest management (IPM) is an ecosystem-based strategy that focuses on long-term prevention of pests or their damage through a combination of cultural, physical, biological, and chemical controls.

Cultural controls are gardening practices that reduce pest establishment, reproduction, dispersal, and survival, such as growing pest-resistant varieties of plants or adjusting irrigation.

Physical controls are actions that eliminate pests or make the garden environment unsuitable for them, like netting to keep birds out and traps that capture rodents.

Biological controls are natural enemies like predators, parasites, pathogens, and competitors used to control pests and their damage.

Chemical controls are pesticides used to eliminate pests, chosen for their ability to do the job with limited effects on other organisms, air, soil, and water quality.

Beneficial insects are Good Guy Bugs that prey on harmful insects that damage landscape plants or edible crops.

aphids, and caterpillars. Others, like whiteflies, thrips, and slugs, are not so easy to spot. However, not all insects are pests, and to complicate matters, not all pests are insects. Gophers, rabbits, deer, birds, cats and dogs, even humans, all do damage.

Gardens are nature constrained. Within their boundaries gardens function like mini-ecosystems, and other living creatures come with the territory. Insects, birds, and mammals are as much a part of a garden as the plants we grow. Some of these inhabitants are well behaved—friendly in fact, even helpful. Others are disruptive, causing immediate damage or long-term problems that require farsighted solutions. Since pests are sure to visit our gardens from time to time, gardeners must be ready and aware. Identifying a pest problem is the first step toward solving it, and like

most problems, pest problems are easier to solve when recognized from the start.

A good approach to fighting pests is integrated pest management (IPM). Developed in the 1970s in response to the overuse of pesticides, IPM considers the interactions among people, pests, and plants to find the best way to combat pests while limiting risk to humans and the environment. Beyond simple extermination, IPM determines why the pest became a problem in the first place and seeks to control it through an approach that combines cultural, physical, biological, and chemical tactics. It starts with the

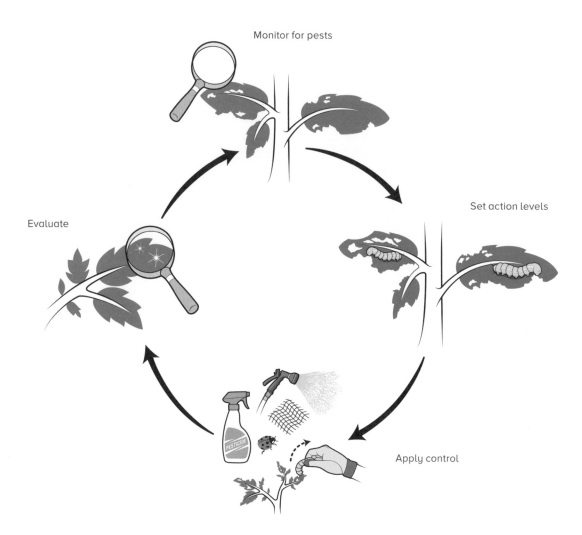

Monitor for pests

Set action levels

Apply control

Evaluate

IPM goes beyond simple extermination.

least harmful and costly approach and escalates only if the problem persists. For example, you would spray aphids off your rose bushes with water first, and only if they persisted would you spray with insecticidal soap.

Step 1: Monitor for pests

The first step in a proactive approach is to recognize an issue before it becomes a problem. Symptoms may appear suddenly or over time, and the purpose of active monitoring is to discover the damage done by pests at the earliest possible moment. With mammals it's relatively obvious,

but insect damage can be more difficult to see, so we must look closely or use traps to find them. The culprit must be identified along with the extent of the infestation before any action is taken.

Spend time in your garden just looking, with no motive in mind other than pure observation of what's there and how it's faring. Pests are experts at camouflage or avoidance, so gardeners must actively search them out by turning over leaves, rustling around plant roots, and examining bark and shoots. Do this at least once a month, in every season, and find a way to make it fun. I enjoy photographing gardens and use the time behind the camera to study my botanical subjects through a practical and aesthetic eye.

INSECTS

Don't be surprised to find any or all of these insects in your garden at some time, though you can hope never all at once. After the first time you find one of these pests, it will be easy to recognize them and the damage they do. Just like the best way to know a plant is to grow a plant, the best way to find a bug is to have fought a bug.

Aphids are tiny sap suckers that reproduce quickly, causing significant damage if left unchecked.

Beetles start as grubs in the ground, where they damage plant roots and then hatch into adults that skeletonize leaves by chewing and sucking.

Caterpillars and loopers chew and eat leaves, and if their population explodes they can completely defoliate a plant.

Aphids

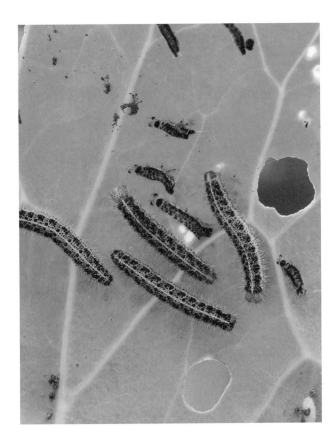

Caterpillars and loopers

Beetles

Fungus gnats

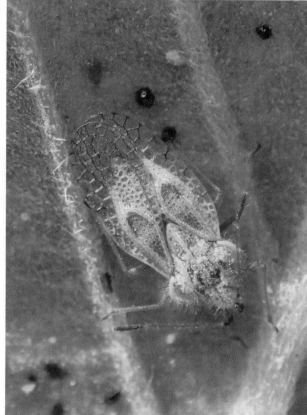

Lace bugs

Fungus gnats pop out around houseplants with soggy potting mix. They are a nuisance but don't harm the plant if present in small numbers.

Lace bugs pierce leaves and suck out the juice, resulting in tiny yellow flecks on the top surface of leaves and dirty brown stains on the underside.

Leaf hoppers suck the sap from piercings made on the undersides of leaves. Their saliva is toxic, causing the foliage to yellow and curl.

Leaf hoppers

Leaf miners

Mealy bugs

Scale

Leaf miners eat the leaves from the inside. Tiny flies lay their eggs in the leaf, and when the larvae hatch they start feeding.

Mealy bugs attach to stems and suck out the sap. As they eat, they excrete a sugary honeydew that promotes the growth of sooty mold, an ugly black fungus, on the leaves below.

Scale insects suck sap from stems and leaves. Once attached they form a protective shell that is difficult to dislodge, so it's usually easier just to remove the infected branch.

Spider mites are related to spiders and make webs that envelop the foliage. They thrive in hot, dry conditions, attacking plants by piercing the undersides of leaves to suck the juices.

Thrips are small and hard to spot, but their sucking and scratching damage is easy to see. Leaves turn splotchy and die, and the entire plant becomes twisted and scarred.

Whiteflies crowd around the undersides of leaves and suck sap. They lay their eggs in the same place, making it necessary to completely remove infested foliage.

Thrips

Spider mites

Whiteflies

Critters can cause significant damage if left unchecked.

MOLLUSKS, MAMMALS, AND BIRDS

Observing wildlife is one of the joys of tending a bit of nature in the form of a garden, but there is a difference between sighting a gentle doe browsing at dawn in an open field and finding her devouring all your rosebuds. Gardeners must strike a balance between protecting plants for their own use and sharing the bounty with local fauna. Whatever your attitude toward these critters, the damage they cause can be significant if left unchecked.

Slugs are terrestrial mollusks that thrive in humid conditions. They come out of the mulch or soil at night to chew on leaves, making irregular holes and ragged margins.

Gophers burrow underground and eat plant roots. **Groundhogs** eat the soft shoots of herbaceous plants and young shrubs.

Moles tunnel just below the surface of the soil in search of earthworms and insects, leaving squishy trails in your lawn. **Voles** tunnel between the mulch and the soil, eating plant crowns, roots, and bulbs as they go. You can spot their winding runs in the early spring as the snow thaws. **Shrews** reuse mole and vole tunnels looking for insects, slugs, and weed seeds to eat, making them friends to the gardener.

Mice rarely cause problems in the garden unless their population explodes in the autumn, which is when they may vandalize your edibles. **Rats** are an urban garden problem, most often encountered when attracted to food scraps in compost piles.

Raccoons could be called suburban rats. They too are attracted by kitchen scraps in your composter and will chew their way into it if they catch a scent of something good inside.

Squirrels chew the bark and twigs from trees and eat their cones and seeds. They may also leave holes in the lawn where they bury their nuts. **Chipmunks** injure plants as they swipe fruits and nuts. They also dig up and eat small spring-flowering bulbs like crocus.

Rabbits most commonly eat the soft shoots of young plants. They don't kill the plant outright but weaken and stunt its growth with repeat visits.

Deer are the bane of many a gardener's existence. They have an uncanny knack for eating flowers right before they open, and the list of what they won't eat is woefully short.

Family pets can wreak havoc in the garden if left unrestrained. Dogs trample beds and dig holes, and their urine burns plants. Cats have a nasty habit of pooping among the vegetables and flowers.

Birds don't damage so much as steal, harvesting fruits, especially berries, just as they ripen. It's typical for a blueberry bush to be stripped clean in a single morning by rapacious waxwings or robins.

Step 2: Set action levels

The type of pest and the extent of the infestation determine the seriousness of the problem. It's up to the gardener to decide to what extent the pest can, or should, be tolerated. One groundhog is one too many, while a dozen aphids barely rate. It depends on how much damage is being done and also the persistence of the pest. If it is causing cosmetic disfigurement but no permanent harm to plants, let it be but remain vigilant. If affected plants are dying, something must be done to slow or solve the problem, keeping in mind that the best gardening practices are

A good blast of water from a hose often works to wash unwelcome insects off of leaves, although it doesn't guarantee the death of the pests.

always the least intrusive. Optimistic gardeners approach pests philosophically, considering losses a natural consequence of working with nature, and striving for a balanced ecosystem in support of human needs.

Step 3: Apply controls

Actions that specifically protect our gardens from pests are called controls. The best overall strategy consists of four types of controls working in concert: cultural, physical, biological, and chemical. Using just one type of control probably won't get the job done, while using a combination of two or more most likely will. Cultural controls are the foundation, and the level of intervention and toxicity rises as each of the other kinds of controls are applied successively. Always consider potential consequences to the environment before employing any control.

Cultural controls Everything it takes to grow a healthy, unstressed plant—such as following the "right plant, right place" mantra of plant selection, supplemental watering and fertilizing, and selective removal of excess or infected detritus—is considered a cultural control. Plants naturally release hormones that ward off pests, but when a plant is stressed it has fewer resources to make these hormones. Like a wolf pack targeting a slow or injured animal, pests attack weak plants. Fundamentals such as pruning and proper spacing of plants also promote a healthy environment.

Physical controls Fences and netting are obvious physical controls we use to keep out mammals and birds; floating row covers made of Reemay and held down around the edges with soil or rocks can keep bugs off veggies. Sticky traps work. Try a homemade version made from an index card slathered with petroleum jelly but avoid pheromone-based traps that tend to draw every targeted pest in the entire neighborhood to your garden. The simplest way to handle mild infestations is to pick the bugs off your plants and kill them directly. When I find a slug, I toss it on a sunny sidewalk where it writhes and dies. Or I use beer to lure and drown them.

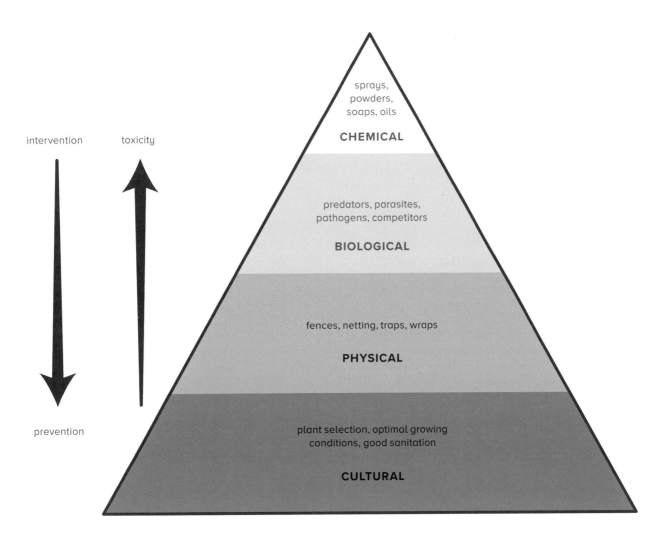

The four kinds of controls can be thought of as a pyramid, with cultural controls
forming the foundation and chemical controls the capstone, to be used sparingly if at all.

How to Deter Animal Pests with Physical Controls

Animals pay no heed to our efforts to create beautiful, productive gardens. In fact, the better the garden the more likely it is to attract animals. These visitors don't mean to upset us with the damage they do—they're simply following instinct, so don't blame them. Instead, be smart and limit their interest or access by deploying repellent sprays, strategic fencing, wraps, and traps.

Repellent sprays come in many odorous forms, including rotten egg goo and lemony oil laced with pepper. They all work on the premise of discouraging animals, such as deer, groundhogs, rabbits, and house pets, from eating plants by making them taste bad or camouflaging them with a masking scent. The trouble comes when the gardener neglects to reapply the spray consistently, so set a spray schedule and stick to it, rain or shine.

Fencing works only if properly designed, installed, and maintained. The height and depth of the fence is of prime importance. Deer will easily jump anything lower than an eight-foot fence, and a groundhog will burrow beneath it, so set the height right and dig wire fencing in at least two feet deep. The cost of fencing your entire property can be prohibitive, so apply it strategically: around edible plots and cut flower beds, and also to protect susceptible ornamental plantings and shrubs during lean seasons when wild forage is scarce.

Wraps help protect plants from animals when the plants are at their most vulnerable, such as the tender bark of a newly planted tree or rows of peppers and beans ripening in a vegetable garden. Simply covering the plant is enough to confound the critters.

Traps shouldn't be cruel but must be effective. It could be argued that a spring trap that kills the animal instantly is the most humane way. Live traps like the Havahart trap, a cage with a door that shuts when the critter enters it to get at the bait inside, catch the animal unharmed but raise the question: Once it's caught, what do you do with it? Transporting the critter some miles away and releasing it into the wild is illegal in most places. Whatever you do, research and obey all state regulations for catching and releasing wildlife.

Biological controls Biological controls use the pest's natural enemies against it. Predator insects can be purchased and released into the garden, but after all their prey is eaten they will leave in search of more, and you'll have to buy them again if the pest returns. A better strategy is to keep the ecology of your garden in balance by promoting habitat for good insects that eat the bad ones.

Symbiotic relationships between plants and insects, where each supports the other, are common in nature. A holistic approach to gardening takes advantage of these relationships and fosters self-supporting ecosystems in our home landscapes. This may consist of growing specific plants or allowing some detritus like leaves and logs to rot in place as habitat for beneficial bugs.

Chemical controls Chemical controls (target-specific, low-toxicity pesticides) should be used only if all other controls are ineffective and maybe not even then. Chemical controls come in different forms based on the material being used and the effect we want it to have on the pest.

- Foliar sprays work on bugs that live on the stems and leaves of plants, either killing them outright or when they eat coated plant parts. Sprays also make foliage unpalatable to animals like rabbits and deer.

- Powders are dusts that work like foliar sprays but don't require a spray pump to apply. They last longer and don't wash off as easily, which allows the ingredients to continue working. Simply shake the powder from a can onto the plant shoots. Do it on a windless day, taking care to keep it off your skin, and wear a mask so you don't breathe it in.

- Systemics are used to kill pests living inside the plant where foliar sprays and powders can't reach. Usually diluted and applied to the soil, they are absorbed by the plant and kill the bug inside.

Be skeptical of chemical pesticides advertised as "safe." Past products commonly used but subsequently banned were nerve agents developed for war, diluted and sold for use on insects. With continued use the active ingredients in pesticides build up in the environment, posing health risks to humans and wildlife. Most pesticides kill more than their target pest—they also kill beneficial bugs. My advice is to stay away from synthetic pesticides and use organic options instead. Here are some organic options proven to work:

- Insecticidal soap is sprayed on the infested plant. It penetrates soft-bodied insects and kills them.

- Horticultural/dormant oil is sprayed on the infested plant. It smothers the insect—the eggs in the case of dormant oil—and kills it.

- Rubbing alcohol applied on a cotton ball or swab wipes bugs like scale off of stems and leaves, killing them in the process.

- Boric acid is a powder sprinkled on the ground where insects eat it and die. Don't get any on the plants or they will dry out and die too.

Beneficial Insects: The Good Guys

A garden with a balanced ecosystem provides its own biological controls. You can also buy the help of some Good Guy Bugs.

- Ladybugs eat soft-bodied insects like aphids, mites, whiteflies, and scale.

- Assassin bugs prey on a variety of pests, including flies and caterpillars.

- A praying mantis when young eats aphids, leafhoppers, mosquitoes, and caterpillars, then graduates to beetles, grasshoppers, and crickets when it matures.

- Predator wasps lay their eggs in the eggs of pests, like whitefly. When the wasp larva hatches, it eats the whitefly egg.

- Beneficial nematodes are microscopic worms that feed on insect pests. They are so small they can enter the plant and attacks pests like leaf miners on the inside.

- Milky spore isn't a bug, it's a bacterium that kills beetles in their larval stage. Commercialized as a product you can buy and apply, it's popular among organic gardeners.

- Diatomaceous earth is a silica powder made of fossilized plankton, or diatoms. These microscopic-sized shards of glass cut into insects and kill them.

- Kaolin clay is a powder used to make porcelain. It makes edibles inedible to pests but can be safely and easily washed off.

- White vinegar mixed with water and sprayed around—but not *on*—plants (it's also an herbacide) doesn't kill the bugs but does act as a repellent.

The Life Cycle of an Insect Pest

Insects go through several stages during their life as they metamorphose into adults. Eggs are laid on plants or in leaf litter, where they hatch into larvae. These then feed on the host plant or the detritus on the ground. The larvae, or grubs, change into nymphs, which are small versions of the adult. Some insects pass through several nymph stages, called instars, before they reach adulthood and are ready to reproduce.

While they may inflict damage on our plants throughout their life cycle, bugs are usually most vulnerable to controls at only one time during the cycle, typically the larva or nymph stage. For example, Japanese beetle adults are impervious to treatment, but when they are grubs living in the soil, they can be effectively eliminated with beneficial nematodes or a target-specific bacterium powder.

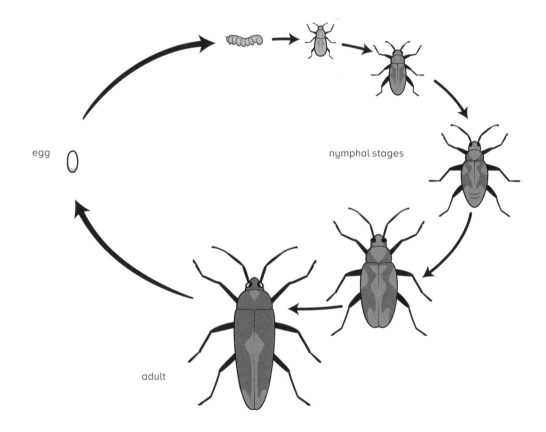

egg

nymphal stages

adult

Insects go through a life cycle from egg to larva to nymph to adult, and one of those stages will be the optimal time to strike.

Which type of control to use is determined by the pest problem, and the best way to develop a treatment strategy is to know your enemy. For insects, this means finding out when they are most vulnerable and timing attacks accordingly. The best specific strategy is always the least hazardous to humans and the ecology, the most likely to be permanent, easy and safe to apply, and cost effective.

Step 4: Evaluation

The final step in IPM is a visual check for the persistence of the pest and a health assessment of the plants. These observations provide valuable information for ongoing treatment, allowing for modifications to the strategies you've applied. The ultimate goal is the elimination of the pest with no, or minimal, adverse effects on nontarget species. If the problem isn't solved, you may need to consult with a professional. In any case, be flexible and fine-tune treatment from year to year and pest to pest.

Diseases: A Good Defense Is the Best Medicine

Bugs attack weak plants, and so do diseases, making the best defense against disease your ability to grow strong, healthy plants in a living soil. Gardens propped up on synthetic fertilizers, herbicides, and pesticides are unsustainable and ultimately collapse. The challenge of gardening is to strike a balance between human interaction and nature's guidance, providing healthful conditions for plants and preemptively treating for diseases only when appropriate.

Never put diseased plant parts in the compost. The compost will be contaminated, and if it's spread on beds, the disease will spread with it.

Preventing diseases

Keeping diseases from developing in the first place is the best course of action. Follow these suggestions and you may never need to diagnose a disease in your garden:

- Grow a diverse mixture of disease-resistant or disease-tolerant plants.
- Match plants to growing conditions of sun, soil, and climate.
- Avoid overhead watering and proactively prune to increase air circulation in beds.
- Control disease-transmitting pests, and weeds that harbor pests and disease.
- Sanitize tools and keep the growing environment clean to stop diseases from spreading.
- Remove and destroy diseased plants. Bag them in plastic and toss them in the trash.

Categorizing the ugly: Three types of disease

Plant disease is caused by three main types of pathogens: fungal, bacterial, and viral. The most common are fungal diseases, but they are also the easiest to prevent. Bacterial attacks occur less frequently but are difficult to control, while viral infections are least common and can't be cured. All three produce symptoms on roots, stems, leaves, flowers, and fruits.

Fungal problems are caused by minute organisms and spread most often by way of water, wind, and insects. They can be prevented by spraying susceptible plants with a sulfur fungicide—which is safe for use around humans, birds, bees, and fish—just as new growth emerges. Target the tender shoots of herbaceous plants as they emerge from the ground, and buds on trees and shrubs just as they begin to open. A springtime inoculation should protect the plants through the season, but a second application in the middle of a wet summer is a shrewd preventative measure.

Powdery mildew

Botrytis is common on many flowers, fruits, and foliage, causing affected areas to turn black, shrivel, and die. Cut off the infected parts and the rest of the plant will be fine.

Powdery mildew is found on many garden plants, especially where overhead watering is used. Powdery gray or white patches on leaves reduce photosynthesis, so over time the plant weakens and may die.

Rusts are ugly growths that start as rust-colored flecks and grow into bumps. They weaken their host plant, often resulting in premature leaf drop, gradual decline, and early demise. Rust diseases are spread by spores transferred from infected plants to healthy plants, most often in mild, moist conditions.

You can make your own antifungal spray by mixing a tablespoon of baking soda, a tablespoon of vegetable oil, and a few drops of dishwashing soap with a quart of water. Spray on healthy leaves of at-risk plants but be aware that too much may burn them.

Botrytis

Rust

Bacterial infections are caused by single-celled organisms and spread by wind or splashing rain, insects, and even birds, producing symptoms of rot, wilt, and spots. Preventing wounds where bacteria enter the plant and using resistant cultivars are the best ways to avoid bacterial attacks.

Cankers affect the leaves, stems, and fruit on trees. Conditions for the bacteria are favorable when high temperatures and excessive rainfall coincide with early shoot development. To keep cankers from spreading, remove infected parts or the whole tree if the infection persists.

Blight can develop anytime, but cool, wet weather is most favorable for the disease. A spell of hot, dry weather clears up the problem, but it will return with the next rains. Once again, disposal of the infected plant is the best remedy.

Cankers

Blight

Wilts

Viral assaults are parasitic, meaning the virus infiltrates plant cells, using them as a host. This disrupts normal cell growth, resulting in deformed leaves, stems, and fruits. Insects are the main source of viral infections, though unsterilized pruning tools can also transmit viruses from plant to plant.

Wilts are often transmitted by thrips and are common on tomato and pepper plants. The leaves soon wilt, die, and fall off and the pest moves on to another plant, making diagnosis of thrips as the cause difficult. When fruits are infected they may remain intact but display unhealthy skins.

Mosaics often occur on rose bushes, causing the leaves to turn colors in unique patterns resembling their namesake. This is primarily a cosmetic issue, but if the changes are extensive, photosynthesis can be affected and the plants will weaken.

Mosaics

Nitrogen deficiency

Potassium deficiency

Nutrient deficiencies that look like diseases

When a plant looks sick, the issue isn't necessarily a pest or disease. It could be a nutrient deficiency in the soil. A sudden or gradual color change in a plant's foliage might mean the plant is malnourished. Less consequential than any pest or disease problem, deficiencies in the three macronutrients (nitrogen, phosphorus, and potassium) as well as the trace element iron are easy to deduce and correct with fertilizers.

Nitrogen deficiency is marked by a complete yellowing of leaves.

Phosphorus deficiency shows up as a purpling of leaves from the margins in.

Potassium deficiency is indicated by a yellowing from the margins in.

Iron is deficient if leaves turn yellow but midribs and veins are green.

Iron deficiency

How to Diagnose a Plant Problem

There are several ways to figure out from the symptoms what condition or disease a plant is suffering from. One way is to refer to a copy of *Home Gardener's Problem Solver*. This is a thick volume filled with disturbing photos of every nasty disease seen on plants. I warn my students that since a chemical company publishes this book, nearly every remedy proposed includes using one of the many products manufactured by that company. I suggest they use the book only to identify the issue and then do further research on remedies.

I prefer consulting online sites and forums, like missouribotanicalgarden.org and davesgarden.com, but they work best when you start with some clues. The best resource is your local garden center or university extension office. Experienced gardeners there will be able to recognize diseases easily from a sample stem or leaf you bring in.

Phosphorus deficiency

Nontoxic, eco-friendly controls keep your garden in balance with nature and safe for visiting pollinators, like butterflies and bees.

What to do for ailing plants

Dealing with disease is difficult because unlike pest problems, once a disease takes hold there is often no cure. This is especially true for herbaceous plants. Woodies may survive for a while, but in most cases, a premature death is imminent. Most treatment is meant to keep the disease from spreading to neighboring plants. This involves completely removing the sick plant from the garden, bagging it, and tossing it into the garbage.

Choose organic (nontoxic) controls over synthetic (toxic) ones whenever possible. The extent to which each is useful depends on the plants you grow and the type of garden you want. Raising hybrid tea roses or fruiting apples typically requires the use of some chemicals for consistent success. Native plants and disease-resistant cultivars need less help to perform their best. Most important, learn to manage expectations. Every organic gardener expects to find a blemish or bug on tomatoes or cabbage. If you want perfectly formed fruits and vegetables like you would find in a chain grocery store, be prepared to break out the chemicals.

Your approach to handling weeds, pests, and disease should reflect your horticultural outlook and intentions. Some gardeners cannot bear the sight of a single weed or damaged leaf, while others revel in what the Japanese call wabi-sabi: the art of imperfection, which includes an appreciation of nature's cycles of growth and decay. Personally, I enjoy the serendipitous adventure of give and take between gardener and nature characterized by an imperfect garden. Professionally, however, I am often tasked to attain some level of perfection in the gardens I create and care for. Garden as you see fit, making your garden a reflection of your own spirit. Remain true to your garden and it will be true to you.

afterword

Gardening Provides

The moment you decide to grow a plant, you awaken the potential gardener within yourself. That's just the beginning. Gardening, for most, is not a passing fancy but a lifelong passion that drives us to grow more and learn more. It's my hope that this book has ignited that passion and awakened the intuitive gardener within you.

It happens as you realize how plants live and grow and reproduce, and when you make the connection that the soil is actually alive. From there the gardening tasks of planting, mulching, watering, and feeding fall into place. You understand why gardeners do what they do and why what they do doesn't always work. Confidence builds as you practice pruning and confront weeds, pests, and diseases, realizing all the while you're becoming a true gardener.

These moments of realization as you apply the lessons and practice the skills you have learned in this book herald your entry into a flow of gardening experiences. This flow is your life in gardening. Deep thoughts from a simple gardener, but that's the attraction. From a flower to a smile: gardening provides.

Happy gardening!

—Daryl

Acknowledgments

This book was a long time coming. For years my students at
the New York Botanical Garden have lamented the lack of a single,
all-encompassing introductory text to supplement the lecture material in my
Fundamentals of Gardening course. This text would not exist without them,
because they were my first audience. Long before I had any students, Gool and
Dinyar Wadia took a chance on an aspiring gardener from Wisconsin and hired him
as head gardener on their estate, Gitaljai, where I learned to grow. Two decades later,
they and their head gardener, John Horn, invited us to photograph the garden where
it all started so we could include it in this book.

Equally important were two decades of clients who let me practice gardening in their
gardens: Rob Sollmann, Jim Richards, and Julie Stevenson, to name just a few. Thanks
also go to the publishers and editors at *Horticulture, Fine Gardening,* and *Martha
Stewart Living,* who helped me polish my writing skills over the years and actually paid
me to share my knowledge and passion for all things gardening on the pages of their
magazines. A particular thank-you to Jessica Dodell-Feder for teaching me the
difference between a gardener and a "yardener."

My affiliation with the New York Botanical Garden played a central role in the genesis of this book. My deepest gratitude must be expressed to everyone at NYBG, especially Lisa Whitmer and Barbara Corcoran. Lisa was the earliest adopter of my plan to write this text, and her encouragement and enthusiasm was invaluable.

Thanks too to Barbara Jones, a great friend and the first to suggest I should teach gardening.

A special shout-out goes to Michael Blakeney and Brian Sisco for opening their garden to multiple photo shoots so we could capture many of the images on these pages. Thanks for those photos goes to Bryan Gardner, and for his talent, experience, and good-natured attitude. Thanks also to his assistants, Hadley and Martyna, who were models of patience on those long days in the gardens. Equally understanding and ever helpful, Will McKay at Timber Press must be congratulated for shepherding this book and its untried author from a rough idea to a completed work. Will introduced me to Lorraine Anderson, eco-editor extraordinaire, who molded a manuscript into a masterpiece. Thanks also to designer Adrianna Sutton and illustrator Kate Francis for bringing these lessons to life on every page.

Deep thanks are due my family: Carrie, for laughing it off when my in-laws asked why she was marrying a "farmer," and my sons, Simon and Leo, for keeping me grounded and in the garden.

Further Reading

Adams, George. 2013. *Gardening for the Birds: How to Create a Bird-Friendly Backyard*. Portland, OR: Timber Press.

Armitage, Allan. 2011. *Armitage's Garden Perennials*, second edition. Portland, OR: Timber Press.

Baldwin, Debra Lee. 2017. *Designing with Succulents*, second edition. Portland, OR: Timber Press.

Brown, George E. 2009. *The Pruning of Trees, Shrubs, and Conifers*, second edition, revised and expanded by Tony Kirkham. Portland, OR: Timber Press.

Capek, Karel. 2002. *The Gardener's Year*. New York: Random House.

Capon, Brian. 2010. *Botany for Gardeners*, third edition. Portland, OR: Timber Press.

Cruso, Thalassa. 1971. *Making Things Grow Outdoors*. New York: Knopf.

Damrosch, Barbara. 2008. *The Garden Primer*, second edition. New York: Workman.

Darke, Rick, and Doug Tallamy. 2014. *The Living Landscape: Designing for Beauty and Biodiversity in the Home Landscape*. Portland, OR: Timber Press.

Dirr, Michael A. 2011. *Dirr's Encyclopedia of Trees and Shrubs*. Portland, OR: Timber Press.

DiSabato-Aust, Tracy. 2017. *The Well-Tended Perennial Garden*, third edition. Portland, OR: Timber Press.

Gershuny, Grace. 1993. *Start with the Soil*. Emmaus, PA: Rodale Press.

Halpin, Anne Moyer, and the Editors of Rodale Press. 1990. *Foolproof Planting*. Emmaus, PA: Rodale Press.

Lowenfels, Jeff, and Wayne Lewis. 2010. *Teaming with Microbes: The Organic Gardener's Guide to the Soil Food Web*, revised edition. Portland, OR: Timber Press.

Mitchell, Henry. 2003. *The Essential Earthman: Henry Mitchell on Gardening*. Indianapolis: Indiana University Press.

Nardi, James B. 2007. *Life in the Soil*. Chicago: University of Chicago Press.

Ogden, Scott, and Lauren Springer Ogden. 2011. *Waterwise Plants for Sustainable Gardens: 200 Drought Tolerant Choices for All Climates*. Portland, OR: Timber Press.

Perenyi, Eleanor. 2002. *Green Thoughts: A Writer in the Garden*. New York: Random House.

Smith, Miranda. 2007. *The Plant Propagator's Bible*. Emmaus, PA: Rodale Press.

Snodgrass, Edmund C., and Lucie Snodgrass. 2006. *Green Roof Plants: A Resource and Planting Guide*. Portland, OR: Timber Press.

Snodsmith, Ralph. 1993. *Ralph Snodsmith's Fundamentals of Gardening*. New York: Morrow.

Stearn, William T. 2004. *Botanical Latin*, fourth edition. Portland, OR: Timber Press.

Tallamy, Doug. 2007. *Bringing Nature Home: How You Can Sustain Wildlife with Native Plants*. Portland, OR: Timber Press.

The Timber Press Regional Vegetable Gardening Series (*The Timber Press Guide to Vegetable Gardening in . . .*). Various authors and dates. Portland, OR: Timber Press.

Turnbull, Cass. 2012. *Cass Turnbull's Guide to Pruning*, third edition. Seattle, WA: Sasquatch Books.

Photo and Illustration Credits

index

f

g

y

z

Daryl Beyers is gardening certificate program coordinator at the New York Botanical Garden, where he helps shape the education department's curriculum, and teaches the popular Fundamentals of Gardening course. He has had more than twenty-five years of professional landscaping experience, specializing in residential garden design and development. As a staff writer, photographer, and editor for *Fine Gardening* magazine, he authored two special issues on garden design, and he served as contributing garden editor for *Martha Stewart Living*. His articles on gardening and garden design have also appeared in *Horticulture* and *HGTV Magazine*. He maintains an active speaking schedule throughout the year, presenting at a wide variety of garden shows and clubs across the country, both independently and on behalf of NYBG.